Professional Training for Feminist Therapists: Personal Memoirs

Professional Training for Feminist Therapists: Personal Memoirs

Esther D. Rothblum
Ellen Cole
Editors

Routledge
Taylor & Francis Group
LONDON AND NEW YORK

First published 1991 by Haworth Press, Inc.

Published 2018 by Routledge
2 Park Square, Milton Park, Abingdon, Oxon OX14 4RN
52 Vanderbilt Avenue, New York, NY 10017

Routledge is an imprint of the Taylor & Francis Group, an informa business

First issued in paperback 2018

Copyright © 1991 Taylor & Francis

All rights reserved. No part of this book may be reprinted or reproduced or utilised in any form or by any electronic, mechanical, or other means, now known or hereafter invented, including photocopying and recording, or in any information storage or retrieval system, without permission in writing from the publishers.

Notice:
Product or corporate names may be trademarks or registered trademarks, and are used only for identification and explanation without intent to infringe.

Professional Training for Feminist Therapists: Personal Memoirs has also been published as *Women & Therapy*, Volume 11, Number 1 1991.

Library of Congress Cataloging-in-Publication Data

Professional training for feminist therapists: personal memoirs/ Esther D. Rothblum, Ellen Cole, editors.
    p. cm.
    Published also as v. 11, no. 1 of Women & therapy.
    ISBN 1-56024-123-3 (acid-free paper)
    1. Women psychotherapists – Training of – United States. 2. Women psychotherapists – United States – Biography. 3. Feminists – United States – Biography. I. Rothblum, Esther D. II. Cole, Ellen.
RC459.5.U6P76 1991
616.89'14'082 – dc20
                                            90-26555
                                              CIP

ISBN 13: 978-1-138-98389-2 (pbk)
ISBN 13: 978-1-56024-123-2 (hbk)

Professional Training for Feminist Therapists: Personal Memoirs

CONTENTS

Preface *Esther D. Rothblum* *Ellen Cole*	xiii
Feminist Therapy as Family Tradition: A Mother and Daughter Support Each Other's Growth as Women *Naomi B. McCormick* *Marcelle R. Adolph*	1
Double Margins: Woman and Psychologist *Julia Sherman*	17
How Feminism Changed My Life and World View *Hannah Lerman*	27
From Penis Envy to Goddesses in Everywoman: Revising Theory to Fit Experience *Jean Shinoda Bolen*	35
My Personal Education as a Feminist Therapist *Judith J. Frankel*	55
Thinking Together *Michele Clark*	63
From Black Person to Black Female to African-American Woman: A Critical Developmental Transition for a Feminist Therapist *Robbie J. Steward*	71

Courage in the Trenches 79
    Toni Napoli

On Remaining a Radical Lesbian Feminist While Training
  in Psychiatry 91
    Laura L. Post

Feminism and Psychology: A Dangerous Liaison 103
    Six Spoke Collective

Graduate Training and Feminism: Maintaining an Identity 111
    Melissa J. Perry

ABOUT THE EDITORS

Esther D. Rothblum, PhD, is Associate Professor in the department of psychology at the University of Vermont. She is currently a Kellogg Fellow and has travelled to Africa to study women's mental health. Her research and writing have focused on mental health disorders in which women predominate, including depression, the social stigma of women's weight, procrastination and fear of failure, and women in the Antarctic. She has co-edited six books, including *Another Silenced Trauma: Twelve Feminist Therapists and Activists Respond to One Woman's Recovery from War,* which received a 1987 Distinguished Publication Award from the Association for Women in Psychology. Dr. Rothblum is a co-editor of the journal *Women & Therapy* and co-editor of the Haworth Series on Women.

Ellen Cole, PhD, has devoted 25 years to the practice of psychology. She is currently an adjunct faculty member in the Human Development Program, Prescott College, Prescott, Arizona. An AASECT certified sex therapist and sex educator, she was formerly a professor of psychology at Goddard College in Vermont and chair of the Committee on Women and Minorities of the Vermont Psychological Association. In addition, she co-edited, with Esther Rothblum, the book *Another Silenced Trauma*, which received a 1987 Distinguished Publication Award from the Association for Women in Psychology. Dr. Cole is a co-editor of the journal *Women & Therapy*, co-editor of the Haworth Series on Women, and mother of four young adults.

∞ ALL HAWORTH BOOKS & JOURNALS
ARE PRINTED ON CERTIFIED
ACID-FREE PAPER

Professional Training for Feminist Therapists: Personal Memoirs

Preface

Professional training for feminist therapists—a contradiction in terms? Over a year ago, we asked feminist therapists to write about their own training as feminists and as therapists. What was it like becoming a feminist? What was it like undergoing training as a therapist? Which came first? What were the professional/personal/ethical dilemmas along the way? How did the professional training influence current practice today?

What follow are personal memoirs from seventeen women. Two women, mother and daughter, both therapists, one trained in the 1930s and one in the 1970s, reminisce to each other about their professional training. One woman writes about entering graduate school in the 1950s, at a time when women in her psychology graduate program were prohibited from specializing solely in research, since there were no academic positions for women. Another woman describes her psychoanalytically-oriented graduate program before she was aware of feminism. Another is raped in her home and years later enters graduate school in order to work with clients who have been sexually abused. One woman enters a counseling graduate program during the politically conscious 60s. Another writes about sabotage of her teaching by the old-boy network. One woman describes the experience of coming out as a lesbian in medical school and during a psychiatric residency program. Another woman writes about the double minority status of being female and Japanese-American. One woman enters graduate school comfortable with her identity as Black and female and has to confront the alienation and invisibility of her presence in an all-White classroom. Six women who are currently in graduate school describe the dilemma of evolving as feminists while concurrently developing as psychologists. And a woman who is in her first year of graduate school describes the transition from a women's studies undergraduate focus to a traditional research institution.

© 1991 by The Haworth Press, Inc. All rights reserved.

The accounts that follow are that combination of painful memories, active struggle, impromptu friendship, and humor that have become so familiar to women as we struggle for professional development without eliminating our own identities. The memoirs appear in order of years of graduate training, from earliest to most recent. Nevertheless, there are more commonalities across the years than differences, as even current graduate students describe feminism as an alien concept in their training.

It was impossible to read these memoirs without thinking of our own training. Esther had completed her Ph.D. at age 25, had mostly male mentors and was encouraged to publish early on in her career. It wasn't until her internship that she met other feminist graduate students and began to write about her research areas from a feminist perspective. Her mentors, concerned, advised her to discontinue her focus on women "for the sake of her career." Fortunately she disregarded their advice for her professional work now focuses entirely on feminist research, editing, teaching, and community activism.

Ellen dropped out of a prestigious doctoral program, with an all-male faculty, in her mid-twenties because she was pregnant and her husband had accepted a job in another state. Eleven years and four children later she completed her doctoral work at a "nontraditional" institution, with a wonderfully supportive and competent female faculty advisor, and became licensed to practice psychology in Vermont. At about the same time, she read *The Second Sex* and *The Feminine Mystique* and was jolted forever into a new reality. However, even personal history repeats itself. Twenty-four years after the first move, she has once again re-located to a new state because of her husband's job, and has just been rejected for state psychologist certification. She is pursuing legal action, and is aware that she has encountered yet another women's issue.

Some women are unable to speak about their experiences. A graduate student gave us permission to quote the following from her letter: "After much consideration and three anxious months of writing and discarding worthless drafts, I regret that I cannot accept your invitation to submit an article. Each attempt to write a personal memoir about being a physically different woman and an ethnic minority in clinical training resulted in a disappointing outcome. I have been struggling with a way to present my experiences without crossing the boundaries of damaging self-disclosure. Unfortunately, I could not strike a comfortable balance between what I wanted to reveal in print, while protecting my person, yet remain true to the goals of the special issue."

We respect this woman and other women who cannot currently speak about their training without furthering their pain or risking their careers. At the same time, it is our hope that many women who read these articles will be moved to record their own experiences, for the clarity and insight that comes from reflection, and for the sake of women who will undergo professional training in future generations.

Esther D. Rothblum
Ellen Cole
Co-Editors

Feminist Therapy as Family Tradition: A Mother and Daughter Support Each Other's Growth as Women

Naomi B. McCormick
Marcelle R. Adolph

MARCELLE'S STORY

What do I think, Naomi? I think that one doesn't become a feminist suddenly after a flash of insight. Instead, feminist consciousness is the result of the merging of personal values with those of family, friends, and community. The books you and I read, our teachers, the groups we belonged to, and perhaps for me more than you, Jewish identity—all have played a critical role in both our decision to become therapists and our embrace of feminism.

At age 76, this is a time when I am consolidating my memories, trying to make sense of many, varied experiences. Thinking about my education as a feminist is part of that process. I can trace the beginnings of feminist consciousness to early childhood when I noticed how my parents, Jewish-Polish immigrants to the United States, treated me differently from my brother. From age four on, I

A Fellow in Rational-Emotive Therapy, Naomi B. McCormick is Professor of Psychology at the State University of New York at Plattsburgh where she received an award for teaching excellence in 1988. Aged 41, she is Co-Chair of the Feminist Interest Group of the Society for the Scientific Study of Sex and has published widely on the relationship between sex roles and sexual behavior.

Marcelle R. Adolph, Naomi's 76 year old mother, continues to be an active social worker after retiring from Rush Presbyterian St. Luke's Medical Center, Chicago, where she was recognized as Employee of the Year in 1975. Presently, Marcelle serves on the Board of Directors of both the National Council of Jewish Women in Evanston/Skokie, IL and the Chicago Metropolitan Battered Women's Network.

was expected to be the nurturing sister, taking care of my brother who was only two years younger than I, assuming responsibility when he got in trouble at school or one of us had to mind the family business. At age 12, my caretaking duties expanded to looking after my mother who had a difficult menopause. Frequently, I had to miss school to assume these duties. Fortunately for me, my teacher made a home visit and ordered the family to return me to school.

It now seems callous to me that no family member cared whether or not I attended school. Perhaps, these early memories somehow influenced me when I became a parent. I was determined not to do the same thing to you, my daughter. I did my best to let you know that there is more to life for girls and women than taking care of others. Maybe that is why you are so achievement-oriented and independent. Who knows? Naomi: Do you recall a cardboard wardrobe just your size to store your clothes? You were three years old. Anyway, you would decide each day what you would wear. You seldom accepted my suggestions. Do you remember how much difficulty you gave me when I tried to teach you piano at age five? You wanted to be autonomous even then; you didn't want lessons from me.

In a recent telephone call, I shared an experience that we both had at around age five. Each of us had boys we liked to play with. In my case, I was very close to the grandson of a businessman down the street from my parents' jewelry store; you were close to twin boys who were neighbors. I remember when you said that you had "married" David and Dennis. As I recall, the two boys escorted you with a doll carriage after the wedding ceremony in our pantry. Even then, you demonstrated a budding interest in sex research and sex education! Anyway, both you and I were forbidden from continuing our friendships with boys. One day, each of us was told by the boys' families that our friendships were inappropriate, that little girls were not supposed to play with little boys. We were both heart-broken. Early on, we learned that girls and women were discriminated against, separated from boys and men lest we "contaminate" them with our femaleness.

When I grew older, my father (your grandfather) had me read Emerson's essay, "Self-Reliance." This had a strong influence on me throughout my life. During early adolescence, my father reinforced the message of the essay by telling me that marriage is important but could not be depended upon. He urged me to be able to support myself by earning a living. My father's economic concerns were prophetic; he died when I was 18 and the family jewelry business went into bankruptcy. My earnings in the Work Progress Administration (WPA) supported my mother, aunt, younger brother, and me during the height of the Great Depression. Being a caretaker for my extended family surely taught me the importance of economic resources for women and prepared me for the social work profession.

I don't want to ignore your grandmother's, great-grandmother's, and great-aunts' roles in preparing us to become feminists. My grandmother (your great-grandmother) ran the family business in Poland while her Orthodox Jewish husband studied the Talmud in the synagogue. My mother (your grandmother) had the courage to divorce a man she had been paired off with in an arranged marriage after immigrating to the United States from the Old Country. She then married my father (your grandfather) after which the two worked side by side in the family jewelry store which was located in a working-class neighborhood in Chicago. The silent movies at the local theater served as daycare for my brother and me when we weren't minding the store. None of your female elders on my side of the family were homemakers. Three of your great-aunts (my mother's and father's sisters) worked outside the home from late childhood on in the retail, hairstyling, and seamstress trades. Can you remember when I told you about Aunt Rose's lover in France, her squabbles with the garment workers' union leadership, and her firm belief that "marriage is a form of legal prostitution?" You did not come from the conventional American family.

Two images of my mother as a strong woman remain vivid in my memory. As a young woman, she refused to shave her head and wear the "shetl" (the ceremonial wig required of devout Jewish women) during her first, unsuccessful marriage. She was proud of her beautiful, long, chestnut, wavy hair. My father, her second husband, used to enjoy watching her brush her hair each evening. Yet, she was eager and willing to crop her hair into the short, comfortable, "flapper" style during the Roaring Twenties despite his objections. Her head belonged to nobody but herself!

Our family has had a long history of radical political involvement. This and my early work experiences also laid the groundwork for feminism for both of us. Both of your grandfathers were socialists; my brother encouraged me to join the radical youth movement of the 1930s. Questioning the status quo and the power of a privileged few has been part of our family tradition for at least three generations. I can still remember the nurturance of my mother, preparing food for all my brother's friends who volunteered their time at the *Midwest Record*, a left-wing Chicago newspaper published on a shoestring budget.

My desire to do something about social injustice was inspired by the human suffering I witnessed as a young woman, stimulated by the social unrest of the times. In the midst of the Great Depression, I traveled by bus as a representative of the American Youth Congress, founded by Eleanor Roosevelt to help unemployed youth. The poverty and racial injustices I observed during my travels through the coal mining communities of Pennsylvania and the Black ghettoes of Washington, D.C. shall remain etched in my memory forever. Fortunately, I was given an opportunity to become an advocate for the poor and oppressed when I became a group worker at Hull House, our nation's pioneering settlement house, during the late 1930s. Community organizing in the impoverished immigrant community, in the tradition of the famous social workers at this agency founded by Jane Addams, helped me to realize my potential as a woman. Employed initially as a youth recreation worker for the Works Progress Administration (WPA), it was here I was first told I should attend college. A scholarship loan from this agency plus your father's poker earnings during his World War II military service enabled me to earn my B.S. in Group Work Education from George Williams College in 1946. In fact, Hull House has a romantic place in my heart; it was there I met your father whom I married in 1941.

Like many women, I worked in war plants during World War II, coming to appreciate the struggles of women factory workers from the standpoint of direct experience. The 1940s were exciting; I did organizational work for the United Automobile Workers and other progressive groups. During the war years, I chaired the Congress of Industrial Organizations (CIO) Union Canteen which provided recreational services for visiting military personnel in the Chicago area. It was then I attended CIO Canteen College where I learned the history of the American Labor Movement and women's contributions to unions in particular. I was pleased the classes were conducted by both women and men.

You grew up seeing me at work. Your dad and I did not adhere to the 1950s cult of female domesticity. He did as much childrearing and housework as I did during much of your childhood and adolescence. I remember when you were a tiny girl who would dance in my classes at the psychiatric hospital for World War II veterans. Do you remember my work with youth groups at neighborhood centers? You were my harshest critic at the Jewish Community Center day camp. Field trips and projects had to be pretty special to get a good review from you. I can still remember how much fun it was to lead a bus-load of kids in games and song, looking out over the crowd and seeing you smiling at me.

Can you recall when your father and you supported my decision to go to graduate school full time when you were still in elementary school? Those were demanding times, struggling along on one income. I remember how you would read my textbooks to me while I ironed. You were still in the sixth grade but had many insightful questions. You certainly got a head start in the human services field. Do you remember when you spent the day with me in my graduate classes at the University of Illinois, Chicago? At age 11, you took notes just like the older students; you were a great hit.

Certainly, I don't want to paint an overly optimistic picture of my feminist development. The rough period was just after you, my only child, were born. I could no longer work full-time and became very depressed as a result. I went into therapy and had a rude awakening when my female therapist claimed my resentment of my current isolation and my husband's more active outside life in union activities and full time employment was the result of "penis envy." Her interpretation really made me angry; I refused to accept it. My feminist consciousness was heightened when I told her that the issue was not that I wanted to have a penis but that I was opposed to being confined by traditional sex roles. Fortunately, my therapist was open to feminist ideas. She listened to me empathically, supported my point of view, and enabled me to move out of an awful depression and a part-time job I had grown to despise.

I am the kind of person who needs to be involved in the community and work to feel whole and happy. Lucky for me, you were the kind of youngster who supported this at a time when the model for motherhood was a full-time homemaker, ready with milk and cookies when the children returned from school. You learned to be self-reliant and I counted on you to do your part in the family. When you were 10, you no longer would allow me to have baby-sitters around. So, you became a pioneer latch-key kid who looked after yourself competently after informing the next door neighbor of your arrival home from school. Remember when you started a fad in your class? Whether or not their mothers worked, every other child wanted a key on an attractive chain around their necks, like your own, because you were so fashionable.

I think our family's radical traditions fostered feminism in both of us, too. Remember when all three of us marched in favor of nuclear disarmament during the 1950s before this cause was popular? I found this great photograph of you, as an elementary school girl, carrying a huge "Peace Now" sign with your father, the parade marshal, standing at your side beaming. We've been in many marches together. A highlight for me was the massive Equality Day rally in Chicago where together we celebrated the fiftieth anniversary of the passage of the Nineteenth Amendment in August 1970, just before you left for graduate school in Los Angeles. What a sense of continuity!

Thanks for telling me about your favorite feminist books when you were an undergraduate at Roosevelt University. It was fun reading together. Remember when I lent you my copy of *The Second Sex*? I think you still have it. There were so many great books in the 1970s on feminist issues like *Sisterhood is Powerful*, *Against Our Will*, *Sexual Politics*, *Women and Madness*. Who could remember them all? It was fun attending the feminist lectures with you while you were an undergraduate in Chicago, too.

In any event, you know about our mutual voyage into the feminist literature and feminist politics. What you may not remember is how I came to be a feminist therapist. Back in the early 1960s, I grew tired of youth work. I wanted to work with adults and especially with women. Fortunately, I found an interesting position at the Chicago Foundling Home. While working with pregnant adolescents, I began to conceptualize a feminist approach to treatment. This approach developed further during my lengthy career at Rush Presbyterian St. Luke's Medical Center which followed.

During my years at Rush Presbyterian St. Luke's, I encouraged the welfare mothers I worked with to organize and fight for their rights. Such advice proved to be far more effective in treating their depression than conventional psychotherapy. While you were at graduate school, I began using "herstory" and consciousness-raising techniques with my women patients in the psychiatric day hospital. I had learned about these techniques in continuing education classes in local universities. So many of my patients had been sexually and physically abused by their fathers and husbands. A feminist approach seemed essential to help them recover their sense of power. I was delighted when my article, "The All-Women's Consciousness Raising Group as a Component of Treatment for Mental Illness" was published by the journal *Social Work with Groups*, in 1983 just prior to my retirement. You see, it is never too late to get your first publication!

When I retired from Rush Presbyterian, I had no intention of giving up feminist social work. I continue to be involved with many grass-roots women's organizations in Chicago. As you know, I am a board member of the Chicago Metropolitan Battered Women's Network. The "herstory" remains an important facet of my life; I have just completed a herstory of the Chicago Battered Women's Network and look forward to its publication. Presently, I co-edit the newsletter of the National Council of Jewish Women of Evanston/Skokie, also serving on this organization's board of directors. It seems like I have belonged to N.O.W. just about forever. I feel like my feminism continues to evolve. Right now, I am especially concerned with Jewish feminism and have learned a lot from attending seminars conducted by the Women's Division of the American Jewish Congress. For me, Judaism, feminism, and political activism nourish each other.

It is exciting for me to watch your own growth. During my last visit, we switched roles. Instead of me taking you to work, you took me to work. Your father and I enjoyed sitting in on your classes and participating with your students. I especially appreciated your classes on rape and sexual harassment in the workplace. I was proud when I watched you try to raise the feminist consciousness of your students. And thanks, too, for those presents for my 76th birthday; I really love the books—*The Tribe of Dina: A Jewish Women's Anthology* and *A Portrait of American Mothers and Daughters.* The symbolism isn't lost on me. May we continue to grow as individuals and together as feminist therapists!

NAOMI'S STORY

Mom, you have covered most of the early experiences which shaped my feminist consciousness so well that there is little I could add. Here are a few recollections that seem relevant, however. Do you remember how difficult early adolescence was for me? Because our family was less affluent than others in our neighborhood, I didn't have the stylish, expensive clothes that many of the other girls flaunted. Their sarcastic remarks were painful for me. I desperately wanted the straight hair that was in vogue but you insisted that my kinky, curly hair was beautiful in its own unique way. Around that time, I was rejected from a clique of popular girls because our values were discrepant and I had become outspoken. Throughout this period, I questioned my worth but you and Dad stood by me. You pointed out that it was more important to be true to oneself than to please a group and that often the nonconformist was right. You also showed me how it was wrong for girls and women to judge themselves and others based on appearance, clothing, and other superficialities. As I watch so many women suffer because they don't think that they have the right body or physical image, I get in touch with how grateful I am for this feminist instruction.

Thank you, too, for accepting my rebellion against family values later in adolescence. In hindsight, it is amusing to remember how I questioned our progressive family's values by joining conservative youth organizations. First, there was Junior Achievement or Young Capitalists as we jokingly would refer to it later. Here, I was able to become a leader in my one-dollar-a-share company by selling products to neighbors and learning bookkeeping, becoming a popular leader in our regional center by breaking records for the sale of dance tickets. Junior Achievement gave me an opportunity to observe barriers to female achievement early on. The young men I interacted with carefully explained that while I might be a competent vice president of our regional center, I could never be president since "girls were too emotional."

And then there was my stint in my high school's chapter of R.O.T.C. I can still see my uncle's (your brother's) shocked expression when I came to breakfast in my R.O.T.C. uniform. Despite our family's long history in the Peace Movement, I joined R.O.T.C. to get out of gym and most of all to be with my girlfriend who was returning to school after a leave of absence for a mysterious illness that we all suspected was an unwanted pregnancy. But, I couldn't control my budding sense of female autonomy; I took to wearing a button which proclaimed "End the War in Vietnam" on the lapel of my uniform. Moreover, the male officers tried me for "insubordination" because I had delegated a busy-work task to male sergeants (class officers) whom I believed I out-ranked. During my court martial, the young male lieutenant colonel accused me of giving orders to "superiors" since despite my status as first lieutenant, I wasn't "a real officer" because "I was a girl." Throughout adolescence, you and Dad supported my exploration of all the possibilities, ideologically and organizationally. Through positive and negative experiences, I learned to question girls' and women's expected place in society, firming a feminist consciousness while still an adolescent.

Next came the political adventures of college. You and Dad knew all too well about my politics. You were the ones who went to court or picked me up at the police station when I was arrested for this demonstration for student power or that demonstration against the war in Vietnam. You supported my attempts to become a student leader during my undergraduate days at Roosevelt University. Remember how proud you were when I was elected to the Student Senate?

I know you remember when I was falsely convicted of "obstructing traffic and disturbing the peace" during a student peace march and sent to Cook County Jail after the judicial system mysteriously lost their records of my appeal to a higher court. My one night in jail, surrounded by poor women and women of color, was a radicalizing experience for a budding feminist. I shall never forget the traumatic body search and the indignity of being inspected for sexually transmitted diseases in an involuntary, gynecological examination. I remember the prison uniform and being treated like a number and not a person. I remember the stench and fear; the insect infestations in my cell; the shame of no privacy for visiting the toilet. I remember fainting after the humiliation of the body search and gynecological exam, helped to my feet by a caring Black woman who was a fellow inmate. Powerfully, I was made aware that feminism must address the needs of all women, not just the needs of a White, affluent group.

Dad's and your own emotional support during this terrifying period of my life in the summer of 1970 shall always be cherished. Mom, I remember when you took off work to attend court with me every day, supporting me with your empathic eyes during the ordeal. That was more than my so-called steady boyfriend could do. When you asked my boyfriend to accompany you to the jail to pick me up when those in charge were forced to admit that I should not be incarcerated, he said he couldn't come because he might miss a session with his analyst who would interpret it as "resistance." Like you, I also had a direct experience with the oppressiveness of orthodox psychoanalytic ideas. Woman-to-woman, you lovingly confronted me with my boyfriend's lack of support. You helped give me the strength to terminate a lop-sided relationship with a self-absorbed young man. I became determined to select my future partners very carefully, to enjoy solitude, and to develop more appreciation for the reliable, nurturant company of women in my life.

Thank you for respecting my activism. I learned some of the same lessons from the New Left that other women did in those days. On the positive side, I learned that organizational work could lead to constructive social changes. On the negative side, I learned that the barriers to women were strong, even within the so-called radical groups of the times. Like the other women, I typed and duplicated the leaflets and did the tedious work. The men never allowed me to assume a role of real leadership unless being a token woman at a ceremonial conference with the college president meant anything. By the late 1960s and early 1970s, I was getting fed up. I vividly remember attending a political rally with a boyfriend and surprising both of us by getting up and leaving with a feminist caucus. I wasn't sure why I walked out but I knew that I had to walk out. I was aware of my anger but could not yet articulate it. This was a time for reading with you and going to feminist programs. We were learning together about feminism.

Then there was sexuality, an issue that was harder for us to discuss than politics. Those were times when parents hid their sexuality from children and children did likewise. I believe that my continuing interest in sex research and sex education has its roots in adolescence and young adulthood. I knew I was interested in sex but I sensed that the rules for sex, the scripts, were biased against girls and women. I liked a particular girl a whole lot in late elementary school. We used to walk home daily; I admired her courage and intelligence. Then, one of the boys in my class warned me not to hang out with her because she had "a bad reputation," like somehow I would be tainted by being with her. To this day, I get angry when I think about the double-standard of sexuality. I remember the 13 year old boys saying contemptuous things about the girls who were "easy feels." I remember how embarrassed one boy I knew was when my kiss was more aggressive than his own. I also remember how angry I was at a high school boy who explained I was "the kind of girl you liked to be with but didn't want to show off to the guys."

Later, there were the college days, the young men's apartments with black lights and "free love" posters. Free love for whom one might ask? They would brag about their former conquests or try to build up a young woman's ego by comparing her with some inferior conquest. If they were having difficulties with arousal or erection, why that would be the woman's fault too. There was a young man at my college lunchroom who would go into great detail about the breasts of each woman who was entering the vicinity, as if I should be as fascinated with such facts as he was. There were lines and games and hurts. It was a time to learn that women could be relied on for friendship and support much more reliably than men. Toward the end of my undergraduate days, there was a gang of us women who would interact with men largely to compare notes, complain, and make jokes. We were fed up with the love desperadoes who couldn't tolerate our individuality or outside relationships and the love exploiters who looked at us like pinball games.

Then there was graduate school, a time for more growth. It was off to the University of California, Los Angeles (UCLA) in 1970. I am so grateful to a core of fellow women students there. I used to be self-effacing. Every time I said something, I would diminish its importance by saying "This is nothing but . . ." or "This doesn't make much sense but. . . ." They put me on a behavior-modification program during which they would yell in my face "STOP" every time I initiated one of these self-disparaging remarks. They cured me!

Next, there was the required group therapy during our second year of study in the clinical psychology program. The group was led by a rather ineffectual male psychologist who used much of the time to explain how he had "grown out of his marriage" to a wife who had sacrificed herself to his educational progress and career. The male students in our group spent a lot of time being defensive. Talking about feelings was about as easy in this group as it might be in a football huddle. Slowly but surely, through a process none of us can quite explain, we women took over the group. We talked about menstruation, over and over, weekly, and in great detail. The men quit the group. Our therapist remained interested as a voyeur but we dismissed him from the group too. We became a women's group; we met at each other's homes and talked about the really important things.

Next, one of my female clinical supervisors told me about a real consciousness-raising (CR) group. It was 1971 and such groups were very innovative at the time. It was a CR group just for women therapists. Some of us were seasoned therapists and others, like myself, were students. The leaderless agenda, the norm of not questioning another woman's experiences, and the fluid membership were exciting. Our inability to handle a hostile member, destructive group process, or a dominating person in the group was scary.

Some of my women friends became active in Radical Therapy at the time, a feminist version of transactional analysis. I enjoyed going to their collective meetings and participating in open groups that included anyone from the community who wanted help. I liked the Radical Therapy structure of asking group members what they came for, making the agenda for treatment more explicit than in the male-dominated schools of therapy.

I remember when a bunch of us, all women graduate students, collectively taught a community psychology class under the supervision of one of the few women on the UCLA psychology faculty at that time. We adopted the Radical Therapy approach for running our staff meetings for course instructors; we were experimenting with feminist, collective models of leadership. I liked the way the approach addressed emotional needs of members at the same time that tasks were accomplished. I continue to think that this is one of the major contributions that feminists have made to education and treatment.

Leadership experiences in feminist work groups had a negative side, too. I began to learn how my desire to nurture other women could become distorted into rescue attempts which in turn led to resentment on my part and reinforced dependency on the part of the women I was supposedly helping. One glaring example of this was an older graduate student who was a member of our teaching team during graduate school. Throughout the school year, she would ask my friends and me to assume her duties at the last minute because she perceived herself as too distressed and ill to do her share. We, in turn, would rescue her, all the while experiencing growing resentment. Eventually, this unhappy, dependent woman killed herself; the group was forced to come to terms with our guilt, anger, and confusion. Fortunately, we received a lot of support from the feminist faculty member who served as our supervisor and mentor. I began to understand the difference between a loving relationship between women and unhealthy dependency, a critical distinction for any feminist therapist to make.

And then there were my clients, the women's issues. So many of our sessions seemed to be devoted to how much they defined themselves in terms of men. Their very existence seemed dependent on whether there were men in their lives and how those men or past men evaluated them. There were so many love junkies or "love slobs" as I later came to understand them when I learned Rational-Emotive Therapy during my 1983-84 sabbatical in New York. I wish I could go back and see all those women and help them discard their dependence on male approval. I am doing my best to make up for lost time now, using all the cognitive-behavior techniques I picked up from Janet Wolfe and Albert Ellis.

My idea of successful treatment is when women can appreciate the pleasures of their own company and that of other women, fighting their strongly learned tendency to drop everything for the sake of a "relationship" with a man. How costly it is for women to do what is expected, sacrifice everything for male approval! I have seen women emotionally and physically abused at the altar of male approval. I have seen them waste their lives looking for Mr. Right or pursuing Mr. Wrong. The bisexual and lesbian clients in my practice also face oppression from female, sex-role socialization. Fears of rejection by a partner or rejection by their families and the larger community frequently interfere with their personal development and intimacy. Sometimes, however, my clients teach me more than I teach them; it is invigorating to work with self-affirming women who reach out to friends and partners lovingly, without sacrificing their autonomy.

But, I am forgetting my own central relationship with a man here. I have been married nearly twenty years to a man I met in graduate school, a man who has often put my own career and comfort before his own and through some miracle, failed to learn most of the masculine games our society expects. Thanks, John, for empathically listening to all my complaints about men during the early years of our relationship. Thanks for continuously supporting my feminism and independence, standing by the women when our male colleagues and friends talk or behave in a sexist manner. Thanks for coming here for my job and changing your career so I could stay. Thanks, too, for doing most of the housework and trying your best to adopt a woman's approach to sharing feelings and working on relationships.

Feminist therapy is certainly a core aspect of my identity. But, I am a feminist researcher and scholar much more than I am a therapist. Until my last two years of graduate school, I saw my strengths as social and emotional more than as intellectual. I was fully preparing to be a full-time therapist. Then I met two inspiring, young women faculty members who became the co-chairpersons of my doctoral dissertation committee. Mine was the first nearly all-female doctoral committee in psychology at UCLA. And, I got excited about my dissertation on sex differences in young people's strategies for seducing a partner or rejecting a partner's sexual advances. At last, I was getting even with the young men in high school and college who thought women should be sexually passive and naive; I was studying them.

The publication of my dissertation in *Psychology of Women Quarterly* (1979) was the beginning. Since receiving my PhD in 1976, I have been on the faculty of the State University of New York-Plattsburgh. I began working here when our Women's Studies Program was just beginning, when the college president didn't even know what Women's Studies meant. Now, our program has become one of the strongest, cross-disciplinary fields on campus; the women's studies forum is a therapeutic weekly experience for all of us.

Here at SUNY-Plattsburgh, my research has flourished thanks to the enthusiasm of my student collaborators and faculty friends. Here, I first started writing to colleagues doing similar work, a networking experience that led to editing the (1983) book, *Changing Boundaries: Sex Roles and Sexuality*, with a woman colleague from another university who continues to be a dear friend and admired colleague. Empirical and theoretical studies of sexuality, using a feminist model, continue to excite me. Best of all, I have met so many wonderful friends and pioneering researchers in the process. Together, many of us have become active in the feminist interest group of the oldest organization for sex researchers, the Society for the Scientific Study of Sex (SSSS). With my friends' encouragement, I became co-chair of the feminist interest group, helping to edit the newsletter, sharing responsibilities with one of my favorite colleagues. And that is how I see myself now, as a feminist researcher continually concerned about the impact of sex role socialization on sexual ideologies and behaviors. Consistent with this goal, I will devote my next sabbatical to the study of feminist voices in sex research and therapy.

Finally, it is important for me to share how my experience as a patient with chronic illness has shaped my development as a feminist therapist in recent years. In a previous issue of *Women and Therapy*, I described some of my work on the sexual difficulties and coping strategies of women with interstitial cystitis. My work in this area is self-therapy; it has been a challenge for me to live with an incurable illness that causes voiding frequency and chronic pain. Interstitial cystitis or painful bladder disease is a rare disease afflicting mostly women. Often, women are misdiagnosed and their genital pain is dismissed as psychological in nature. Up until recently, little research was done. Today, thanks to the Interstitial Cystitis Association (ICA), a woman-affirming, grass-roots organization, increasing numbers of people with this disease are getting help and new treatments are being explored. I am proud to be part of the ICA's self-help, advocacy programs for women, writing a regular column for the group's national newsletter on how to cope with chronic illness. Therapists, including many feminist clinicians, sometimes exaggerate the extent to which psychological difficulties create or exacerbate health problems. Doing this is a disservice. Through personal experience, I have learned that it is essential for feminist therapists to recognize that women are sometimes victimized by a male-dominated medical establishment and that the experience of illness and disability can foster growth as well as contribute to emotional problems.

Through the years, I have learned that feminist therapists must embrace social activism. Empathy for clients, even a theoretical grasp for how they are oppressed as women is not enough. The truly feminist therapist must challenge sexism, racism, and insensitivity to poor and disabled persons outside of the consulting room. Successful treatment does not produce well-adjusted women. Rather, it encourages women to engage in political organizing, growing as individuals while they assist in the liberation of their sisters. Thanks for teaching me these lessons, Mom. I hope to continue your legacy with clients and students, my surrogate daughters.

Double Margins: Woman and Psychologist

Julia Sherman

Writing this memoir was more difficult than anticipated. To be useful, it needed to be frank, but publication of private experiences is uncomfortable, and there is always the chance that someone else might be embarrassed; this I have tried to avoid. The memoir describes several anecdotes ("click" experiences) because it was such as these that changed my thinking and motivation. This is not to deny the effect of mundane, modal sex-role interactions. They had powerful effects, especially if they were not raised to consciousness, if they were too threatening to acknowledge, or if they had immutable effects on my life.

EARLY LIFE

Born in 1934, nurtured in the image of Shirley Temple, I grew up in Akron, Ohio, daughter of a political science professor and a gifted mother, little sister of a brother two and a half years older than I. In my early years, we lived near the rubber factories, for which the city was known, but when I was ten we moved near the owners of the factories. Though the schools were better, I was uncomfortable with people so much more wealthy than myself.

I was brought up in the Universalist Church (now merged with the Unitarian Church) and my family emphasized values of social responsibility and respect for others of different religious and social

---

Julia Sherman, PhD, is in private practice in Madison, WI and Associate Clinical Consultant at the University of Wisconsin, Madison. She has been active in feminist causes, especially with the American Psychological Association, and has published widely in the area of psychology of women.

groups. My mother was a feminist and the first President of the League of Women Voters in Akron. Though she had many ambitions, her activities were hampered by ill health. My father commonly pitched in to do the cooking, cleaning, and laundry. He had many hobbies; he was a nature lover and an avid gardener. From him, I acquired a love of nature and sharpened powers of observation. When I was mystified by word problems in the eighth grade, it was he who patiently untangled them for me. He was always fun to be with and took pride in my intellectual development.

When World War II started, my mother entered paid employment for the first time since her youth. She talked her way into a position as employment counselor to the handicapped and her stories about her work awakened my interest in psychology. She quit her job when she became pregnant with my sister, who was born when I was thirteen. Despite this additional responsibility, she persisted in her struggle for personal development. She learned to drive a car, got a real estate license, and graduated from college with top honors, goals apparently modest, but significant accomplishments, given her background and situation.

The second wave of feminism reached her in the form of *The Second Sex*, by Simone de Beauvoir, topic of the University of Akron faculty wives' discussion group. Contrary to her usual custom, she refused to allow me to read the book. Curiosity aroused, I plied her with questions, but her answers were vague and delivered in the same tone she had used when telling me how to put on my first menstrual pad. She told me nothing of sex and I was in my late twenties before I integrated the idea of an abortion.

ADVANCED EDUCATION

I was to fulfill her ambitions. "You can be anything you want to be," she told me, a well-meant but oversimplified encouragement that was to become a motto for women in the seventies. She sent me off to graduate school in psychology at the State University of Iowa in Iowa City saying, "Have a good time, dear," a phrase I was to repeat to the hilarity of my classmates.

My upbringing partly overcame the marry-and-have-children mentality of the 1950's, but I still felt a sense of failure because I had not married upon graduation from college. Though influenced by feminist ideas, I did not integrate them into my life in any consistent way. Put-downs, discrimination, and abuse from men were experienced as individual bad luck or personal failings on my part. For example, in 1955, no women in the Iowa psychology program were allowed to specialize only in research. At that time it was nearly impossible to place a woman in an academic position and the faculty "did not want it on their conscience" that they were graduating women with Ph.D.s who could not be employed. I was grateful to them for protecting us from that misfortune, and it never occurred to me that they might have taken a more active stance. I consoled myself with the fact that I liked clinical work and I planned to get an academic position after acquiring clinical experience, but that was not to be.

Though learning theory was preeminent at Iowa, I obtained an adequate education in clinical psychology. There were no women professors or mentors and I did not expect any. The only special attention paid to the psychology of women occurred during my Post-Doctoral Fellowship at Iowa Psychopathic Hospital in Iowa City. I was advised to read up on the psychology of women. Eagerly I searched for the recommended volumes by Helene Deutsch. Scanning them, I was incredulous that her ideas were taken seriously and disdained to waste my time with such improbable speculations.

During that year, I began my first intensive psychotherapy case, a fifteen year old boy hospitalized on an inpatient psychiatric unit because of emotional problems and ulcers. He had been sexually abused by a male neighbor. (Today he would have been given family and individual outpatient treatment near his home.) In 1958, Rogerian therapy was popular and I did my best to reflect back his statements and feelings. Bobby (not his real name) quickly cured me of this by flying into a rage, fiercely mocking my clumsy Rogerianism. I never used the technique again. Bobby had more rages directed mainly against the head child psychiatrist, Dr. Barnes, who periodically attempted to give Bobby a stern, fatherly talking-to. I did not understand the ominous quality of Bobby's rages and sense of persecution.

After several months of hospitalization, Bobby was discharged and returned to his home on the other side of the state. During one of my last days of training, he returned for a follow-up visit. It was late on a hot summer afternoon and I sat in front of an open, screened window for our last meeting. Without warning, the interview went out of control. He accused me of conspiring with Dr. Barnes to send him to prison. His face was contorted, red and swollen with rage. He threatened to push me out the window. I had always considered him a child, but I now realized that he was much stronger than I and that we were alone in that wing of the hospital. My knowledge of Freudian theory flashed into mind and I said, "You must have done something you feel guilty about." The rage left him like a deflating balloon and he confessed that he had homosexually seduced his younger brother.

The experience of empathy and impotence as I watched the developing terror and rage of Bobby's paranoid schizophrenia dominated the year, yet it held other challenges as well, events important for eventual development as a therapist for women. One of the three interns in the program, Vince, made a point of telling me that Ruth (not her real name) was a lesbian. Ruth was a quiet, steady woman and we had worked well together. Vince urged me to be especially friendly with her. The more he urged, the more alarmed I became. Vince tried to reason with me and out of my mouth came a classic statement of homophobia, "That's all right for you to say. You're a male." Confronted with the raw irrationality of my fear, it faded away and Ruth and I continued our usual, casual relationship.

Though I accepted male homosexuality, it was a long time before I came fully to terms with lesbianism. When my first known lesbian client was filled with rage and could no longer talk in psychotherapy, it never occurred to me to bring up the question of her sexual feelings toward me, a technique I was soon to employ routinely with my male clients.

My understanding of lesbianism grew through my contacts with other women as the Women's Movement began. I lost my phobia, though at first my acceptance was more shallow than I realized since I lacked sufficient knowledge of lesbian experience, like the liberal who accepts Afro-Americans, but has no information about their customs. Reading and more experience were essential to close that gap.

During the late spring of my training year, a wrenching drama unfolded. The third intern, Joan, learned that one of her clients was sexually involved with Dr. Miller, the head of the hospital. She was worried and upset. Within weeks of the revelation she was taken mortally ill and died, Dr. Miller resigned and lost his license to practice medicine in the State of Iowa, and Dr. Miller's wife committed suicide. The swift reaction to Dr. Miller's misconduct left me with a misleading confidence in the integrity of medical self-policing.

Then came the final staff meeting of the year. I was late; entered the room and found there were no chairs. The department head was a kindly man, but now he turned on me. As Dr. Baer, one of the staff psychologists, rose to get me a chair, he said, "No, let her get her own chair. She's going out into the world as a professional. It's time she found out what it's really like." I was dressed in a navy knit suit wearing platform, sling-back, high heel shoes, a form of dress I adopted because he had insisted that I dress "professionally." I found an available chair several offices away. I was dismayed by his unexpected hostility. What did it mean? I attempted to pick up the heavy, wooden institutional chair. There was no way I could carry it. I dragged it, clattering down the hall. I felt humiliated and confused. Women were all right when they looked up to men, but not when they were to become equals.

EMPLOYMENT

After finishing my Fellowship, I took my first job at the Minneapolis V.A. Hospital. An opening developed for a psychologist in the Psychiatry Department at the University of Minnesota. I was refused the job because I was a woman, so I learned from Starke Hathaway, a member of the hiring committee. Starke did what he could, but a powerful member of the committee was dead set against hiring a woman. I was angry, but at that time, nothing could be done.

Restless with the bureaucracy of the V.A., I went into private practice for two years, but I was still restless, seeking an outlet for creative, intellectual energies. Then came a time when I was occupied with marriage and family. It was in the process of becoming a mother that I began to phrase questions about the psychology of women in a scientific form. The breast-feeding and natural child birth movements had begun in California where I was now living. I was exposed to considerable social pressure to do things the new-old way. What did the scientific literature have to say about this? Once the questioning began, it continued.

Next I worked in the War on Poverty; when I refused to hold the boss' hand, I returned the next day to find that I had no desk. I quit and began to write. I was skeptical of what women were being told, of what I was being told and I set out to apply my discipline to the task of a better approximation of the truth.

FEMINIST WORK

Brought up in the half-light of the earlier feminism, events had finally galvanized a personal feminism of my own. As Betty Friedan's book, *Feminine Mystique*, was about to appear, I was writing my own book, *On the Psychology of Women: A Survey of Empirical Studies*, a self-made feminist book of scientific psychology, an assertion of my right to think.

While finishing the book, I began to look for professional work in Madison, Wisconsin where we moved in 1968. My experience was similar to that of many women who try to find appropriate work in a place not of their choosing and where they have no contacts. I finally took a part-time job counseling "unwed mothers." For the first time I had to face the issue of abortion. Our mandate was to allow the client to explore the issues without pressuring her in any one direction. Her choices were abortion, placing the baby for adoption, or keeping the baby. In the course of this work, I observed that women who kept their babies under adverse conditions or placed them for adoption sometimes experienced severe emotional stress. The emotional risk of abortion needed to be considered in the perspective of the outcome of other options. This view found its way into the abortion literature.

Publication of *On the Psychology of Women: A Survey of Empirical Studies* brought me to the attention of national women leaders in psychology such as Martha Mednick, Carolyn Payton, Annette Brodsky, Judy Long Laws, Hannah Lerman, the political scientist

Jo Freeman, the sociologist Jessie Bernard, and the psychiatrist Anne Seiden. Locally important were Corinne Koufacous and Leticia Smith, co-directors with me in the Women's Research Institute, Inc., which we founded. These women and events, more than books, educated and socialized me as a feminist.

My new friends were peer models: Martha's generous trust in my abilities and her judicious manner; tiny Annette's erect posture and resourceful goal orientation; Carolyn's wisdom, sense of fairness yet uncompromising clarity of view; Hannah's rich translation of her therapy experience into a clear, coherent, theoretical form; Jessie's generosity, good humor, and creative insights; Anne's passionate, knowledgeable advocacy for women. The motto was, "Bring a sister," and I was the sister.

I learned by example, by correction, and by insight. Sitting over coffee with the members of the A.P.A. Task Force on Sex Bias and Sex-Role Stereotyping in Psychotherapeutic Practice, we went over a first draft of my writing. Carolyn pointed to the number of qualifying words I had included, the typical, hesitant, weak phraseology of stereotypic women's writing. She struggled with me patiently while I tried to rephrase. I never forgot it.

Meeting Jessie at a conference, she began talking in her wonderful, ebullient style. "Clicks," she said. "Something happens and your mind goes, click." I looked confused. She explained, "Growth in feminist consciousness proceeds by clicks. Suddenly an experience makes you understand something you never understood before." I have based this memoir on a series of such clicks.

Corrine Koufacous and I formed a firm partnership of mutual influence. She had a way of making an idea become a reality and she was fearless. Leticia Smith, always ready to help, lent her incisive mind and cool judgment. Our years together were fruitful and satisfying: writing, editing, giving conferences and doing research, especially on women and mathematics. Part of the time I continued as a therapist, with male sex offenders. With the onset of the Reagan administration, I knew there would be no more funds for our research institute and returned to private practice, specializing in the treatment of women, including collaborative treatment, with psychiatrists, of women with Post-Traumatic Stress Disorder and Major Depression, Bipolar Disorder, or misdiagnosed Borderline

Disorder. There are few women psychiatrists in Madison and male psychiatrists could not treat these women effectively alone. In the future, psychologists may increasingly collaborate with psychiatrists in the treatment of severely ill clients since, despite assertions to the contrary, psychotherapy does have a part to play in their treatment. My most innovative work is the application of feminist therapy to this neglected group of women.

My therapy style evolved depending on what I found useful. Principles of learning theory were a given. Freudian theory, purged by scientific and feminist criticism, was important, especially analysis of dreams which I had learned from Calvin Hall, as an undergraduate. However, I learned most from my personal therapy with Paul Meehl. He reinforced my impression of the power of dream analysis and I learned the value of mutually honest analysis of the relationship. At that time he was influenced by the views of Sandor Rado which emphasized tactical preference for the analysis of the relationship and a philosophy of preventing regression. I adopted these values.

Honesty and respect for the individuality and dignity of each human being was part of my upbringing. It helped me to develop an effective therapeutic stance as a feminist therapist. Naturally empathic and trusting, the trust I extended to clients was returned by their trust in me and in themselves. Self-knowledge and self-comfort from my own psychotherapy allowed me to help clients understand their distortions of me. (Trust and openness, handicaps in dealing with ruthless people, were virtues in dealing with clients.) Coupled with these personal characteristics was my burgeoning knowledge of the psychology of women. This knowledge included sociological analysis of sex roles, ethnic groups, class, and sexual orientation. Specific techniques I used were assertiveness, aspects of Transactional Analysis and Gestalt Therapy, communication and child-rearing skills, and a problem solving technique that looked beyond the woman herself as the source of distress. Clients distressed by the malfunction of someone close to them (vicarious suffering) were helped to do a genuine rescue, though "detaching with love" was a more frequent outcome.

It is beyond the scope of this paper to describe the differential diagnostic and specialized therapy techniques that I use for clients with Post-Traumatic Stress Disorder and severe mood disorders (and often substance abuse or other additional disorders). Here, I can only note some of the controversies, problems, and areas of specialized knowledge I have used in their therapy. The issues are both of a political and substantive nature.

Since these clients are usually women traumatized by men, active therapeutic engagement with clients sometimes places me, with the clients, in the interface of male-dominated power structures. Because of local conditions even medication and hospitalization must usually be obtained through male psychiatrists. Ordinarily I have found ways to negotiate the interface without serious conflict, but not always.

Substantive issues include the question of whether or not clients with Bipolar Disorder (and histories of physical or sexual abuse) benefit from psychotherapy, in addition to medication. It is my experience that they obtain marked benefit from psychotherapy tailored to their needs.

Another question involves their diagnosis. Bipolar Disorder appears to be seriously underdiagnosed, especially among adult survivors of incest. In fact, in many instances the dysfunction of the family may be attributed to Bipolar Disorder among its members, especially male relatives.

The Borderline Personality Disorder diagnosis is often misused with a variety of adverse effects for clients. Those with a missed Bipolar Disorder diagnosis may not have an opportunity to benefit from the specific medications for this disorder. In other cases, the Borderline Personality Disorder diagnosis may be used in ways that are contrary to the interests of the client. For example, this diagnosis may be accepted as a valid reason to effectively deny health insurance, or it may be used to discredit a client in anticipation of the client's legal action. This diagnosis appears to be one of the most stigmatizing in the nomenclature.

Psychotherapy for severely ill women with Post-Traumatic Distress Disorder and Major Depression or Bipolar Disorder requires not only knowledge of these disorders and their psychological treatment, but also knowledge of the appropriate medications, their indications, and effects, and side effects. Education regarding psychotropic medications is a controversial and growing interest in psychology.

Although psychotherapy with these severely ill clients is unusually demanding, these clients are also unusually rewarding, interesting, and creative and, perhaps because they are so ill and neglected, their recoveries bring unique satisfaction.

How Feminism Changed My Life and World View

Hannah Lerman

I was trained and had worked in the field for almost ten years before I discovered feminism in 1971. I had been encouraged by my family to continue my education into graduate school although that support was sometimes tenuous and ambivalent. My mother derisively told her friends that I wanted to become a "career girl." Professors in those days wondered out loud in front of women students whether it was worth their while (and the university's) to train women as psychologists. The general expectation seemed to be that if a woman did become a psychologist, her goal would be to work with children. That was never my wish and I spent five years in graduate school saying "No, No, No" whenever the issue came up, as it did frequently with teachers, supervisors, and even other students.

Most of my fellow students were males and excluded us few women from their social circles. If we worked together well and easily in internship settings, the camaraderie disappeared at holiday and end-of-term parties when their wives were present. Somehow, they implied by their stiffness then that there was something wrong with our being friends. I still remember with gratitude the one male student who didn't act that way. Those parties were very lonely. We few women were terrified of not being able to maintain our place in the program and did not know how to give each other support.

During my time in graduate school, I was married and my hus-

Hannah Lerman is a feminist therapist in practice in Los Angeles. She is a long time feminist activist in psychology and the author of *A Mote in Freud's Eye: From Psychoanalysis to the Psychology of Women*, published by Springer in 1986.

band was also a graduate student, although not in psychology. Before one department party, I recall having to iron his shirt instead of studying for my major general psychology course. He did not actually require it so much as I required it of myself—as a proper wife. When we separated, I was in terror of the rumors he was spreading about the reasons for our separation to his department. I was afraid the rumors would be heard by my professors.

There were subtle things all the time. One I remember most vividly was the action by the teacher of the optional course in hypnosis. He never said I couldn't get into the class but, somehow, I didn't and I don't think that any woman ever did take a hypnosis course from him during my time at school there.

I also sat through classes that dealt with psychoanalytic theory as if it were a factual description of women. I had trouble even at that time with Freud's view of the superego in women as being less well developed than in men. My first attempt at a dissertation project was to try to test this out. Unfortunately, the methodology wasn't good and it didn't work out. I did, however, get some support from one or two male professors (there were almost no women) in this project. At the time, I realized that no one had compared the psychological development material in psychology proper, psychoanalysis, sociology, anthropology, and physiology. That was the impetus for my Freud book when I rediscovered the idea years later.

After graduation, I worked in standard traditional male dominated settings where the atmosphere was even worse. My first job after graduate school was at the Topeka State Hospital which is affiliated with the Menninger School of Psychiatry. I recall case conferences that included heated debates about whether a diagnosis of hysteria was appropriate for a woman if she indicated that she experienced orgasm during sexual relations. I remember one severely disturbed young woman hospital patient who was forbidden from eating in the dining room with other patients because she did not want to tie back her long loose hair. This was in the early 1960s. We did not have patients who admitted in those days to having experienced incest, but we did occasionally have males as patients who had been caught having sexual relationships with their daughters. This was viewed as extremely rare and highly pathological and often discussed in terms of the social isolation of rural Kansas farm life and the unwillingness of their wives to provide them with sex.

In this hospital based (supposedly) on psychoanalytic principles, any disagreement by female staff (at whatever level) was interpreted as representing penis envy or similar psychopathology. Any difficulty that I had was obviously due to my personal problems. The answer that was given to me was to go into psychoanalysis. Although, at the time, I agreed that the problems were only my personal ones, I managed to leave Topeka before having become hooked into long-term psychoanalysis that would have kept me there, as it indeed kept many other people there.

Next, I came to Los Angeles as a budding prefeminist. I had gone through all the requisite training, jumped the necessary hurdles, but something was still wrong. The rewards of acceptance that were supposed to follow were not there. Los Angeles County Hospital was very different from Topeka, mostly in being less theoretical and more practical. With the constant push of more patients coming in the doors, the niceties of theoretical disputes that existed in Topeka were just not possible in dealing with each case. I do recall hearing comments by psychiatric residents pointing out what Freud said and automatically assuming it to be true on that basis alone. Because of the pressured nature of the situation, the power structure was more clear here. Psychiatrists, almost exclusively male, who worked full time, left the hospital at noon. Psychologists, mixed in gender, were generally expected to stay until around 3 p.m. Social workers who were exclusively female were in their offices during all their official working hours, 8:30 a.m. to 4:30 p.m.

I did go into therapy again in Los Angeles, having previously been in therapy in graduate school. My therapist was a male confrontational humanist and I was in group as well as individual therapy. In group therapy, in particular, I was subject to all the projections from the male members of the group, particularly about my hostility, if I spoke up in anything but the most submissive fashion. My therapist criticized my clothing (too bland) and assumed that when I saw his wife come into his office when I was waiting in the waiting room one day that I would automatically have strong sexual transference reactions.

Next, I was involved in the formation of the California School of

Professional Psychology and its beginnings in Los Angeles. We were all psychologists and there were women as well as men. But at the administrative level, the only women were very senior people who had developed personal professional power in other settings. Even so, there were many personal disputes, most of which were between female and male psychologists with "somehow" the males winning. I myself was the third or fourth woman fired. The reason for all such firings seemed to be the males experiencing what they perceived as insubordination and aggression from the females.

At this time, I was taking my first steps into the formal feminist movement. I attended a meeting which planned a symposium for the Association for Humanistic Psychology annual convention on gender issues. Here is where my early thoughts on Freud resurfaced. I wrote and presented a paper entitled "Psychology according to Sigmunda Freud" in a symposium called "The Sexes Today with the Past Recast." It included papers on Charlene Darwin and St. Paula. I reversed the gender on much of Freud and talked of women as the dominant sex. I mentioned the work of Alfreda Adler, Henry Deutsch and Karl Horney. I did my research in the library of the Los Angeles Psychoanalytic Institute and enjoyed the sense of subversion that using their materials gave me as I turned standard psychoanalytic concepts inside-out.

A consciousness-raising group for women therapists began in Los Angeles at about this time. It went on for approximately 18 months and was an incredibly eye-opening and self-empowering experience. Before this time, I had always hovered on the edges of movements and groups, being sympathetic but not really participating. My father was a radical labor union organizer and socialist. He criticized me during my graduate school days for not marching against involvement in Viet Nam. That was in the very early 1960s. My participation in this consciousness-raising group reached me at a very deep level. I felt as though it went down to my socialist roots, integrated that part of me with which I had not previously come to terms, and that I emerged greatly changed and transformed into a feminist activist.

A small group of us formed Feminist Psychological Associates, based on our consciousness-raising experience together, and began to give workshops for other women professionals. Before this time,

I was not really writing professionally but now, empowered, ideas and thoughts began to flow.

I helped form the Committee for Women in the Division of Psychotherapy (Division 29) of the American Psychological Association. One incredibly exciting experience was our first symposium on feminist therapy. I spoke along with Adrienne Smith from Chicago and Ella Lasky from New York. We had not discussed our ideas with each other beforehand. We found that we had independently come to almost identical thoughts. That was my personal experience of the grass roots nature of the feminist therapy movement in those days. The realization that we were thinking along similar lines was very heady and exhilarating.

By now (having been fired by the California School of Professional Psychology), I was in full time private practice. When I moved my office in 1972, I indicated feminist therapy as a specialty on my change of address notices. I was apparently the first psychologist in Los Angeles to do this. It came to the attention of the Los Angeles County Psychological Association Ethics Committee. What was this "feminist therapy" that I said that I specialized in, they asked. I wrote a detailed three page letter (with references). They replied that I had not been unethical but perhaps had exercised poor judgement. They thought that I should have said that I specialized in "Women's Problems." I let the matter rest there, although in later years I have been a bit regretful that I did not pursue the issue with them further.

There were two national feminist therapy conferences which were held in Colorado around this time. Feminist therapy was a growing discipline. Every day, it seemed, more and more women were announcing their participation in the emerging movement and saying the same things all around the country. At one of the conferences, I experienced my first inklings of the tension between those of us who were professionally trained and feminists who were not. Although I had discovered a peer support group in other women generally, and other professional women in particular, it felt peculiar that I was perceived as being part of a power structure (professionals) in which I had never felt accepted in the first place.

Feminism was trying to establish itself throughout psychology and force psychology to look at our new ideas and our new information. The Association for Women in Psychology was formed and then the Division of the Psychology of Women (Division 35) in the American Psychological Association. Every conference and convention was exciting as I met women who were first grasping this new set of ideas. I made dozens of new friends, women who were my friends in ways that no one had ever really been before.

Nobody taught me anything about feminist therapy. I read what there was to read, talked to other women who had begun identifying themselves as feminist therapists, and started to write. My early paper, "What happens in feminist therapy" was originally written for a symposium at the American Psychological Association Convention. It was passed around in what became an almost underground network of unpublished productions by feminist therapists and other feminist psychologists who wanted to share their ideas with one another. At conferences, I was one of the growing number of women who were called upon to talk about feminist therapy.

When I conducted my first women's group in Los Angeles, I learned, for the first time in my professional life, of sexual relations between therapists and clients. One young woman told her story to me and the group. It was the first time she had spoken about her experiences. She came to the American Psychological Association convention in Hawaii in 1973 to tell her story; the Association for Women in Psychology held an ad hoc meeting and sent a delegation to the powers that be in the American Psychological Association and asked for a task force. That task force on sex role stereotyping and sexual abuse in psychotherapy collected the first data on the subject and, slowly but as a direct result, the attitudes toward that behavior began to change in the profession. And I ended up with a subspecialty in a new area that women had created.

I rediscovered my interest in Freud's views of women and began my book which took 13 years to write and was published in 1986. As feminist therapists identified new areas, I experienced "clicks." I began to ask clients about abuse, which I had not done before, and learned just how often it was there. I would estimate that some form of childhood sexual and/or physical abuse is part of the background of well over half of the clients I see.

Soon, those of us who were being called upon to talk about what feminist therapy was became tired of lecturing. We wanted to talk to others who had explored and thought about the implications beyond the introductory level. So, a group of us formed what became the Feminist Therapy Institute. At one American Psychological Association convention, we gathered in Lenore Walker's room and drew up a list of invitees, women we knew from all over the country, whom we eventually asked to come to our first Feminist Therapy Institute conference in 1982.

We met in Vail, Colorado. Fifty women sat in one airless basement room for a weekend while each of us presented to each other. In that marvelous setting, we did not see the outdoors except when we went outside the lodge for Saturday dinner. It was breathtaking, exciting, and monumental. No one wanted to break up into small groups. Everyone wanted to hear what everyone else had to say. In five minute segments, we presented with an additional five minutes for discussion. The topics of each were ones that could have been debated and discussed for days on end. When we ended, we knew that we had to continue and so we have, although no conference since has matched the exuberance of that initial one. As new women come, they say, however, that their first experience of FTI is like ours when we began it.

As I have indicated, I was forever changed by my introduction to feminism. My entire professional life is different than it was before and different, of course, from what it would have become. It has not always been rosy or as exhilarating as the early discoveries of support and connection were. Personal and professional differences and difficulties among women have come to the fore and have to be dealt with. There is no going back, however, nor would I want to.

From Penis Envy to Goddesses in Everywoman: Revising Theory to Fit Experience

Jean Shinoda Bolen

In 1963, as I began my residency, I was unaware that two events in that same year would lead to the women's movement of the 1970's: Betty Friedan published *The Feminine Mystique*, articulating the emptiness and dissatisfaction of a generation of women who had lived for and through others. It was a well-researched, anger-provoking, and thoughtful book, that explained the vague rumblings of unhappiness and discontent that *Life Magazine* and other publications had already noted. There had never been a more pampered, modern-convenienced group of women in the history of the United States—why then the dissatisfaction, why the unhappiness in suburbia? Friedan explained it as the problem with no name "... the core of the problem for women is not sexual but a problem of identity ... a stunting or evasion of growth ... Our culture does not permit women to accept or gratify their basic need to grow and fulfill their potentialities as human beings, a need which is not

---

Jean Shinoda Bolen, MD, is a psychiatrist and Jungian analyst, Clinical Professor of Psychiatry at the University of California San Francisco Medical Center and faculty member of the C. G. Jung Institute of San Francisco. She is the author of *Goddesses in Everywoman* and *The Tao of Psychology*. She is a Diplomate of the American Board of Psychiatry and Neurology, and a Fellow of the American Academy of Psychoanalysis and the American Orthopsychiatric Association, and had been a member of Board of Directors of the Ms. Foundation for women. She is one of twenty-two women in Vivienne Verdon-Roe's Academy Award Winning anti-nuclear documentary "Women—For America, For the World," and is involved in exploring and linking the archetypal and spiritual dimensions of the women's movement, ecology and nuclear disarmament.

© 1991 by The Haworth Press, Inc. All rights reserved.

solely defined by their sexual role." Blowing the whistle on cultural stereotyping, Freudian indoctrination, and media-hype, this book presented ideas whose time had come, ideas which led to an outpouring of repressed anger, the birth of the women's liberation movement, and later to the formation of NOW, the National Organization for Women.

That same year, 1963, President John F. Kennedy's Commission on the Status of Women published its report, documenting the inequalities of the U.S. economic system: women were not being paid the same as men for doing the same job; women were denied employment opportunities and advancement. Recognition of this glaring unfairness would lead to legislative and political efforts to gain economic and occupational equality for women, and would eventually focus on ratification of the Equal Rights Amendment as the means for accomplishment of these goals.

Meanwhile, in the training of psychiatric residents in the 1960's, Freud's views dominated. We were taught that the lack of a penis was the central issue in women's psychology. This lack meant women were psychologically and physically maimed. Believing that she had been castrated, a girl child dealt with the shock by sublimating the wish for a penis in the wish for a child (if she were normal), or she developed a neurosis. If she denied that any lack existed, she was described as suffering from a "masculinity complex." Using complicated reasoning, again having to do with the lack of a penis, psychoanalysis said women have inherently weaker superegos, and are naturally masochistic. (Later when I was asked why I didn't enter the Psychoanalytic Institute, I muttered something about not being *that* masochistic . . . four times a week on the couch until I capitulated, recanted, and admitted, "Penis-envy, penis-envy, penis-envy!" was not for me.) This was my silent-period phase when discretion seemed the better part of valor, if protest merely branded me as having a masculinity complex. It seemed strange to define a woman only in terms of what she lacked in male physical endowment, and to draw psychological inferences from this, rather than to describe woman for what she did have biologically, a uterus or womb in which a baby could grow, a vagina which could accept a penis or be a birth canal, breasts which lactated and could nurture an infant. I thought if Freud had only been a woman in a matriarchal culture, what a case she could have built for womb-envy!

Around the same time, psychiatrists spoke with a certain amount of contempt about "the suburban-wife syndrome," a pejorative, not an official diagnosis. This label described a typical patient in a suburban psychiatric practice: a middle-class woman who was depressed, anxious and unhappy, who probably drank too much and was taking tranquilizers which her doctor had prescribed. She was seen as an unjustified complainer, a woman who had everything she needed to be happy: husband, children, and a nice house in a good neighborhood. Therapy allowed her to ventilate her feelings. While some of these women would eventually see themselves in Betty Friedan's book as victims of the feminine mystique, psychiatrists lagged behind in becoming aware that women had anything to complain about. Many psychiatrists suggested that having another child was a solution to their women patients' problems, which was consistent with psychoanalytic theory.

The idea that a woman might seek more than fulfilling her biological destiny as mother was highly suspect in psychoanalytic circles. Yet here I was, already an M.D., training to be a psychiatrist, drawn to medicine for altruistic reasons (deficient superego notwithstanding). By psychoanalytic standards, this was not a very normal adaptation.

I was taught psychoanalytic theory in a systematic way in required seminars by orthodox Freudians. I also began a "continuous case" in the first year of my residency. I saw a woman with a neurotic diagnosis twice a week, and discussed these sessions for an hour each week with a psychoanalyst, who was my continuous case supervisor. He had me read Helene Deutsch's *Psychology of Women* in order to understand my patient. Deutsch's two-volume work takes Freud's theories on women and weighs them down with further authority and explanation. The childhood realization that she lacked a penis and must have been castrated was an unavoidable trauma for the female (it was like the theological fall from grace, and the blight of original sin): a woman was maimed psychologically by this castration and thought to bear a male child as a temporary sublimation (or redemption). While she was pregnant, she could fantasize that she had repossessed the penis. A post-partum depression might follow the delivery of the baby and the realization that she had had a baby and not a penis.

It would have been different if the neo-Freudian viewpoint of Karen Horney had been part of my introduction to psychoanalytic thought. She was part of the early group around Freud, who way back then presented evidence to support the idea that women had their own particular development—not merely a lesser and defective version of man's. But I was not exposed to Horney's thought. I happened to go from classical Freudian theory to ego psychology, missing not only Horney, but also Clara Thompson, who wrote in the 1940's of the cultural complications affecting women's development. I would much later, in 1973 or 1974, be introduced to the current of feminist thinking in psychoanalysis through Jean Baker Miller's excellent, annotated anthology, *Psychoanalysis and Women*.

Jungian theory was something I could optionally learn in my residency and was not part of the required curriculum. In the only Jungian seminar offered Joseph Wheelwright held forth weekly in a basement conference room. Dr. Wheelwright shared his own experiences and anecdotes. He conveyed his particular flavor of what being a Jungian was about; his analytic work seemed more of the heart than of the mind. He introduced Jung's idea of anima and animus, and promptly differed with Jung; as a warm, extraverted man, who felt deeply about people and causes, he took a little umbrage that, according to Jung, this was done by his anima and somehow not by him. Jung held that there were contrasexual elements in both men and women, that in addition to a feminine ego a normal woman had a masculine animus, which was a composite of male attitudes and opinions, the capacity to be logical and impersonal, and a guide to her unconscious. A man had a male ego, and a feminine anima through which he felt emotionally and related to others; the anima represented both his soul and idealized woman as well. Jung valued the conscious development of animus qualities, which was a positive way of looking at a woman's achievements in the world.

While "who" does "what" within a psyche may be splitting hairs, it was disturbing and strange to consider that it is not me doing the thinking but my animus that is doing it for me (a ventriloquist and his dummy come to mind). However, because of Dr. Wheelwright's attitude and point of view, in my introduction to Jung's ideas, I also learned that they could be challenged. There was not only more heart, there also was more freedom of thought.

In addition there was the meaningful coincidence of synchronicity of the resident-supervisor assignments. I had been assigned two Jungian consultants, and later requested a third. When I wanted to know what the Jungian theory had to say about women, Esther Harding's *Way of All Women* was suggested.

Esther Harding, writing in 1933, is still relevant reading for women today. Her book describes the effect of relationships, work, marriage, maternity, and aging on the inner life of women, who grow psychologically through experience. It was a fortunate introduction to Jungian thought about women because it made sense to me and began with adult experience, rather than focusing on the theoretical beginnings of women's difficulties before the age of five.

When it came to the decision to plumb my own depths by entering an analytic process, I chose a male Jungian analyst in my last year of residency, whom I had come to know as a case-supervisor earlier. At that point in my training, and throughout the three years of my residency, I never had a woman supervisor, never had transference issues raised from a woman psychiatrist's experience. My training never took my being a woman into consideration. Although the women's liberation movement had begun — feminists had demonstrated against the sex-object element of the Miss America pageant, and women's consciousness groups had slowly begun to form — this psychiatric residency, like all others in the midst of the 1960's, was untouched and unaffected. I recall that in one case conference, a male resident quoted a woman who said that "to be a woman in America was like being a Black," as an example of her loose-associations (her lack of logic and poor quality of thinking). No one said anything to the contrary.

After graduating from my residency in 1966, I applied to the Jungian Institute in San Francisco and was accepted. Back then Jungians were not popular. They would become faddish in the mid-1970's, and now are accepted as being slightly more mainstream than fringe within the field of psychiatry. I was the only person to enter the training program that year. Now, the Institute is besieged by excellent applicants.

The Jungians were personally more positive towards women than the Freudians I had known. They waxed enthusiastic over "the feminine" (which as anima was the feminine part of man as well a the feminine in women) which made the Jungian position un-chauvinistic in its values. But there was a stereotypical bias towards the way a woman should act. The Freudians used labels such as "masculinity complex" and "phallic-women"; the Jungians, while theoretically differing as to the how and why of it, would call an assertive woman with strong ideas an "animus-woman," with the same negative connotation.

At this time I began my fascination with the psychological meaning of the myth of Eros and Psyche, through reading Erich Neumann's *Amor and Psyche*, a commentary on the psychological development of the feminine. He was the only Jungian thinker who presented a model for adult women's psychological growth, a model which clearly applied to many women and was helpful to both psychiatrist and patient in understanding the difficulties and tasks that women faced in their lives, and the archetypal underpinnings for this. Several major points, however, did not seem universally true as he postulated. I, for one, did not follow Psyche's tendency to be overwhelmed with each new task; nor was this true for most professional women I knew. Some needed to develop what Psyche (as a pregnant heroine, placing relationship above all other values) began from, as she faced the tasks through which she would grow. Neumann had stated that this myth represented *the* pattern of psychological development for women. Clearly it seemed to me true for many, but not for all.

My interest in the psychological meaning of myths began with the story of Eros and Psyche. It was also the starting point for my thinking about women's psychology from a Jungian perspective.

Towards the end of the 1960's, and into the 1970's, the women's movement was having an impact in psychology and psychiatry. Men experts-on-women got a taste of newly expressed anger from women for what they were saying. Most retreated and left the field of women's psychology to women, which was how it came about that as a young member of the clinical faculty at the University of

California, I was asked to teach seminars on the psychology of the feminine.

In the process of teaching, my ideas about the psychology of women developed. What had begun as Neumann's version of Psyche changed as I added some of my own insights and found myself making omissions and shifting emphasis. Gradually as I taught, this myth became one of the two pathways of psychological development, rather than the only one. I added a complementary myth, based on Atalanta's mythology, which served as a developmental pathway for women who were achievement-oriented, while Psyche represented the traditional, relationship-oriented woman. Each heroine personifies a one-sided woman who needs to grow.

Atalanta was a woman who resembled Artemis, Goddess of the Hunt, who quite naturally did well what men could do, and bested them at that, without being "unfeminine." This myth and its meaning challenged the necessity of attributing qualities in a woman which lead to success in the world to a masculine animus. Psyche, in contrast, is identified with Aphrodite, the goddess of Love. The pitfalls and tasks to grow were quite different for her.

In my personal life, 1970 began a new phase. My first child, Melody, was born, which was a fulfillment of a traditional role, and an initiation into women's experience which had a profound impact on raising my consciousness.

Sixteen months later, when Andy was born, the experience was compounded, and a difficult phase of two-in-diapers began. Although I had been married for four years, I had not been cast into a traditional role until then. I had not even been called "Mrs." except on envelopes. I was either an individual named Jean, or a professional called Dr. Bolen. As a medical student, intern, resident and psychiatrist, my life and my sense of identity were very atypical for a woman.

I had been spared a lot of sex-role stereotyping in my family, had worn blinders about sexism in society until the women's movement, and had been different enough as I grew to not be the recipient of many of the usual woman's role projections about who I was and what I should be capable or incapable of doing. In my family both my physician-mother and business-father clearly meant it when they asked me, "What are you going to be when you grow up?" a question which boys must seriously consider and most girls are never seriously asked. My answer for the longest time was "a lawyer." Probably because I had verbal abilities and a personality similar to my father's, I was drawn to a career that he once considered. Later on in high school, when my friends were dating and living out the anxieties so well presented in Alix Kates Shulman's *Memories of an Ex-Prom Queen* (about dates, how they looked, and how far to go with whom), I was probably living out Alfred Adler's theories of compensating for inferiority feelings, and instead became a national-level competitor in debate and extemporaneous speaking, and a student body officer. Subtle racial prejudice made achievement the place for me to shine in; as a Japanese-American, the same people who would vote me into office would not vote me into the high school social sororities. Later on, reading Carolyn Heilbrun's *Reinventing Womanhood*, I would realize in retrospect what I had in common with the fourteen tenured women faculty members at Columbia University that she studied, and with women in high managerial positions studied by Margaret Hennig and Anne Jardin in *Managerial Woman*. All but one of Heilbrun's fourteen women had close ties to another cultural heritage. Like Hennig's and Jardin's subjects, they came from all-girl families, or were only children, were first-born, or in some way each was in a position to be chosen by her father as "son," which was my experience. It would seem that being an ethnic outsider, who was out of step socially, with a special supportive relationship with my father, helped me become competent in the world.

While I did have a first-born son relationship with my father, I was also in the then relatively unusual and privileged position of having a professional mother who was a source of "You can do whatever you want to" support. As there become more and more mothers with careers, there may soon be a generation of daughters who do not have to be son-surrogates or feel out of step in order to succeed in the world.

Until then, most high-achievement women will continue in a pattern which separates them from other "ordinary" women, which begins when they feel more like their father's daughter than their mother's daughter, since they are not just like mom. When the angry first wave of women's consciousness raising came, it passed over most successful women because they had not been kept down and did not feel oppressed. They had, in fact, gotten ahead in the world with their fathers' support or with other significant males as mentors. Consequently, many successful women did not feel that the women's movement was about them, or that all other women were their "sisters." I know that I didn't, until I was hit by the double-barrelled impact of intellectual evidence, through the profusion of writing by women in the 1970's, and my personal experience which began when I was pregnant.

While I was pregnant, I continued to work up until shortly before each delivery date, letting patients know six months before, and not taking on new people. It was my intent to take many months off and play it by ear when to return. So I interrupted my office practice. I decided to transfer people who needed to see someone regularly, making sure the referral worked out before I left to have the baby, and to work towards termination of work or the choice of transfer or waiting for the others. I wondered what had been written on the effect pregnancy might have on psychiatric patients, and on the transference, and so looked through the literature. I was struck by the silence on the subject, which has since been remedied to some extent by women psychiatrists who have written about their own experiences.

Increased feelings of closeness were generated in some men and women who identified with me because they were parents. Envy and a fear of abandonment were evoked in some patients who were more vulnerable; still others seemed oblivious to my pregnancy.

For me, the experience of pregnancy was a mild altered state in my usual consciousness. Pregnancy seemed to absorb psychic energy. I became more introverted in a "non-Jungian way" — meaning that my inner life hadn't become more active — when I became involved in the inner world of pregnancy. I became biologically introverted, a carrier of new life with my consciousness vaguely at the level of my navel. I tended towards feeling like a rock in the sun, on a riverbank, watching life go by. Focused, problem-solving energy, so usually a part of my psychic life, now required a conscious effort, a boost up of energy. I now had an inner experience which roughly approximated Psyche's, or the traditional woman of which Neumann writes, who must work to sort out priorities to use power, to be focused on a goal. I became acutely aware that two kinds of psychic energy were available to me: one was a taking things in as they came, an encompassing here and nowness; the other, which I could consciously call on, was focused and directed. So that when I was in my office doing psychological work, I was aware of using energy and focus as a conscious choice, instead of allowing myself to just be there.

Then came labor and delivery. In my internship year at Los Angeles County Hospital, obstetrics had been a favorite rotation of mine, chosen for either two or three rotations at the county affiliate, John Wesly Hospital. Here interns delivered all normal deliveries, and called on residents for help only for difficulties or complicated deliveries. I had been on the doctor-side of more than fifty deliveries, and now was about to experience my first from the mother-side of the process. It is a very different experience. My husband was with me in labor and delivery, sharing the experience which was suspended in time, yet so observant of time: how long the contractions, how long the intervals? Like waves cresting and breaking on the shore and receding to build up once more, the contraction waves grew in intensity until it was very painful, yet in between there was nothing, and then another contraction would build up and come. It hurt, I hurt, and in between and afterwards I forgot. I remember what I thought, not what it actually felt like—I remember thinking that it really did hurt, and I remember feeling I was being initiated into a collective women's experience. It did not matter in the least that I was a doctor; I was giving birth like every woman and any woman ever, who had a child. The "I" that was the unique individual me was unimportant. For now I was participating in a miracle as a carrier of new life, as far as human history was concerned, I was an anonymous vessel for continuation of the human species. Somewhere in this experience, I forged an identity with all women, appreciating the personal vulnerability in the face of the instinctual experience.

In the immediate post-partum period, I was aware of the quiet peacefulness of nursing a small infant in the darkness of the night, of the warmth of the moment, and the mother love I felt for this little one. I also got exhausted by the round-the-clock requirements, and was anxious at my inexperience. Contrasting this with the rotating internship at Los Angeles County Hospital, one of the toughest there is in the initiation ordeal of medicine, I decided that, for me, this was harder. At L.A. County, I might be on-call for thirty-six hours and up for most of it, but then I'd be completely off for twelve hours. (The on-call hours were better there than the first several weeks of new motherhood.) Also, I had four years of medical school preparation for the job, and had fellow interns and residents to call on, contrasted with no experience and only one tired husband's support.

I gained new respect for women through this initiation. I also became aware of the requirements for maturity, patience, and unselfishness that parenthood required. I thought of women who were single parents, those who had a child who in any way was abnormal, who were impoverished, or who already had other small children, and I realized the enormity of the task, a lifetime commitment to another person, who would need active parenting for at least eighteen years.

My second child arrived sixteen months later. Even with disposable Pampers, part-time babysitting help and a supportive husband, there was a fatiguing physical drain. The on-going maintenance required to feed, change, bathe the children, straighten up and take care of the homefront was time and energy consuming. I also found that I now always had my antennae up, tuned in to the whimper or cry, so that I could be there to hold, to comfort, or to play with the child, which took a scanning-caring-for-others consciousness which attended to details. Whether it was to pick up the house or to pick up on the emotional nuances, a particular kind of awareness was required.

What then suffered was a lack of time for abstract ideas, a lack of time for reflection, a lack of time to be an individual creating anything for myself. I became aware that though I had considered myself an extravert, that before children arrived I had had a lot of time for myself. With children on the scene, I discovered that I had a militant introvert in my psyche, who required some alone-time for re-souling, reading and thinking.

Even though I did return to practice part-time, months after each child was born I was submerged in the repetitious requirements and energy drain which this period takes, and so could appreciate what the "trauma of eventlessness" was like, which Robert Seidenberg (1973) wrote where every day and every week in most women's lives are filled with tasks which will need to be redone, and all important decisions—from where one lives to what one's standard of living is—are determined by the husband's occupation, and no new risks or challenges occur. One friend once commented that she thought every woman she knew went "a little bananas" when the kids were pre-schoolers.

I then became aware of how my little children seemed to force or behavior-modify me to stay in the tend-to-details state of mind (which stay-at-home mothers seem to be in most of the time). For when I would concentrate my thinking on something, they would invariably interrupt me. For example, if they were playing together quietly in the next room, and I busied myself cleaning the sink or even reading something light, chances were I could continue doing whatever I was doing. If I decided however, to take advantage of the quiet playtime to read a journal or study something which required my focused attention, a minute or two later an interruption would occur. It seemed as if the kids would pick up by ESP when my attentive-to-them scanning for details psychological state was replaced by focused attention which excluded them. My husband also noted this pattern by watching me try to study. One day we decided to try an experiment. I was in another part of the house, deliberately focused on reading theoretical material, and it took less than a minute before little feet came running in to interrupt.

It is not only little children who react personally when the nurturing woman on whom they depend in the environment tunes them out to focus on some concern of her own. Most women, when they stop to think about it, will realize that the men in their lives often start intruding on their focused time. This invariably leads to frictions, because a woman's usual response (unless it is consciously changed) to having her focus interrupted is to be irritable towards the child or man who interrupted, while he or they were probably responding unconsciously to the anxiety created by her withdrawal of caring energy.

From this experience I was very receptive to what I read in Irene Claremont de Castillejo's *Knowing Woman*. Writing as a Jungian analyst, she described "focused consciousness" and "diffuse awareness," as the two modes of mental attentiveness. While this clearly made sense to me, in that it named my own experience, she went on to define these states of mind in Jungian terms: focused consciousness was a masculine or animus quality, diffuse awareness a feminine or anima attribute. While feminism had made me sensitive to labelling human attributes as male or female, the distinction was further significant because anything done by the animus in a woman or the anima in a man, was by definition in Jungian theory, "inferior" and less conscious than when done by the sex to which the quality was assigned.

Watching the intensity with which my then two year old daughter worked on balancing a series of smaller blocks one on top of the other, which she clearly was doing to please herself, I could see that focused, absorbed-in-the-task consciousness was a natural attribute of hers, as it was for me as a child. My obliviousness to everything around me when I read the comics was a family joke; this capacity for concentration gave me a distinct advantage as a student and helps me now as an author.

Several years later in the mid-1970's, I was reminded that diffuse awareness or attentiveness to the feeling and needs of others is not necessarily the province of the feminine. This time by my little boy, who at four would come over and give me a hug when he quite accurately sensed I could use one.

Obviously both sexes can and do use both forms of consciousness. Feminism made me observe and question previously accepted theories and gender labels in psychiatry and Jungian psychology. Through the Women's Movement literature of the 1970's, I learned how oppressive and limiting stereotyped expectations of women could be, and thus wondered how much was inherent and how much had been ascribed to one sex or the other, and once ascribed, limiting.

In physical medicine, *atrophy of disuse* refers to how muscles waste, and bones decalcify when an arm, leg or body is not allowed to function freely or be exercised, until the person is crippled from the lack of use. Classical Freudian theory and cultural prejudices about women, which discounted the potential for achievement, helped perpetuate the psychological maiming which was an atrophy of disuse for women. Opportunity and time are needed to develop innate qualities. If a culture limited women to traditional roles, if she used up all her energies being pregnant, taking care of children, husbands and households, there would be little evidence that she could think creatively, solve problems or be assertive. My own experience with two infants made me feel I had a mind filled with mush.

My reflections on theory and women's predicament continued through the 1970's. As my thinking was influenced by feminism, I saw role limitations and cultural expectations in myself and in the world. The excitement of discovery and anger at oppression went hand in hand. This was a broad view perspective, like seeing the lay of the land from flying over it. But, coinciding in time with this broad view, was the in depth work I was doing with my patients. Therapy went deeper and became analysis. Archetypal patterns became a means of understanding why people got caught in the grip of an irrational emotion, stuck in a destructive relationship, lived out a role which possessed their life, or became obsessed with a person or idea.

In the process of doing in depth analysis, I found Jungian concepts provided a conceptual framework with which I could find my bearings in the psyche. Gradually, from the mid-1960's on, I went from being interested in knowing more about Jungian ideas to becoming a Jungian analyst. In 1974 I was the first woman to be certified by any institute in ten years.

In the Jungian Institute, my colleagues worked in the collective unconscious, that archetypal layer below the personal unconscious. They generally ignored the "outer collective" and were not influenced by feminist thinking; in turn, Jungians were ignored by the women's movement, which was taking aim on some of the more outrageous Freudian theories. Meanwhile, in the mid-1970's, I had become active in the American Psychiatric Association. I was tapped as a "double minority" (racial, as a Japanese-American, and a woman, I was a "two-fer" at a time of Affirmative Action influence) to be on the APA Council on National Affairs. There I found myself affiliating with a small group of men and women psychiatrists with social conscience, whose efforts were directed toward involving the American Psychiatric Association in social and political areas which directly affected the mental health of people. I joined a handful of women psychiatrists who were working together at the national level to influence this male-dominated, prestigious organization (in 1979 it consisted of 25,000 psychiatrists, 89% male). Politically, women psychiatrists were able to make minor gains in representation, and a few inroads in psychiatric thinking on the teaching of the psychology of women, awareness of sexism, rape and battered women, but the overall impact was disappointingly small.

The biggest and most telling disappointment came over the failure of the American Psychiatric Association to support the Equal Rights Amendment by endorsing the national boycott strategy. Annual meetings of over 400 other national organizations were held only in ERA-ratified states. The APA, in three separate referendums, refused to do this. With women comprising an estimated two-thirds of psychiatric patients, and the knowledge that discrimination lowers self-esteem and results in impotent rage and depression, passage of the ERA could be seen as good for the mental health of women: I thought that psychiatric support of the ERA as a preventive mental health measure was analogous to dentists' support of fluoridation as a dental-health measure. This was not to be the case, however, and in the ensuing struggle over holding the 1981 annual meeting in New Orleans, I became a stand-up-and-be-counted feminist-activist, as founder, and co-chair with Alexandra Symonds, M.D. (a psychoanalyst in the Karen Horney tradition) of *Psychiatrists for ERA*. Gloria Steinem joined our effort. *Time* magazine carried the story and I was on the *Donahue Show*, leading a national boycott by psychiatrists of their own organization.

At the 1980 APA meeting in San Francisco, Psychiatrists for ERA scored a stunning success, when the Board of Trustees voted to withdraw the annual meeting from New Orleans in 1981, and instead find a site in a state that had ratified the Equal Rights Amendment. Six weeks later, I was in Washington, D.C., when the Board rescinded this action. That same afternoon, my literary agent called to tell me that the book proposal for *Goddesses in Everywoman* had been accepted by a publisher. On the same day, I thus made two commitments, to lead a boycott of the American Psychiatric Association's next annual meeting, and to write a book about archetypes in women.

In my feminist-activist role, I would see the archetypes or innate patterns of being, and behaving, of motivation and meaning which can be personified as Greek goddesses, enacted in the psyches of others and myself.

For example, when Gloria Steinem came to speak for Psychiatrists for ERA in San Francisco, she became a larger-than-life symbolic figure to many psychiatrists. I saw that she was being responded to as a personification of Artemis the Goddess of the Hunt, the archer with unerring aim, who came to the rescue of women and punished transgressions against them. Some saw her unrealistically as having the power to punish them, to ruin their practices or even cause them to lose grants from the National Institutes of Mental Health.

Within the APA, women psychiatrists were in two camps, which I came to see as reflections of the dominant archetype in them. Women with an Artemis archetypal affinity for sisterhood aligned themselves as supporters of the needs of women patients and the women's movement; naturally they would support a boycott. Women who were archetypally Athena did not, for they were well-mentored, father's daughters who did not consider women oppressed, nor feel themselves part of a sisterhood. For them, the disruption of a professional meeting was objectionable in principle. I could see that the position taken was consistent or true to the two archetypes with focused consciousness, that empower women to reach professional goals. Artemis with her goal-focus, enjoyment of competition, and comfortable peer relationships with men, and Athena with her clarity of thinking, and ability to plan, strategize and make alliances with powerful men are the archetypes that enable women to be successful in medical school and psychiatric residencies. While both archetypes are developed in me, Artemis values predominate, and Athena abilities are used in the service of these values. Thus I would lead a boycott for equality, and be able to think strategy and alliances.

In 1984, *Goddesses in Everywoman* was published. It was a Jungian-feminist point of view, or as I characterized it—a binocular view of women's psychology—that described women as acted on by inner archetypes which are innate, and outer stereotypes which are culturally determined. Both are powerful, invisible forces that act upon us. Consciousness is the tool which can liberate an individual woman from the unconscious tyranny of both.

It was a perspective that described the diversity and differences among women, and the complexity within an individual woman. It was not pathologically oriented, yet accepted that shadow or negative aspects or archetypal patterns come with the positive attributes of each one. It could also be characterized as a compassionate perspective that took the difficulties and advantages of archetype and cultural bias into consideration. It was a book that only a woman with a Jungian background who had her consciousness raised by the woman's movement could write.

In 1989, *Gods in Everyman* was published. The title made it a companion book to *Goddesses in Everywoman*, but in the intervening years, I came to the conclusion that while most of us have a preponderance of archetypes of our own gender, almost every woman has male archetypes within her as well (and vice-versa). One masculine archetype often becomes well-developed. Mine is Hermes, the Messenger God, the communicator and guide of souls, who accompanied travellers and could go from the underworld to the ordinary world or to Olympus. Like the god with wings on his hat and shoes, I love to take off from airports, travel to far off places, bringing information and discovering what is there.

Gods in Everyman describes the effect of patriarchy on men, on fathers and sons, and families. The book also does for men what *Goddesses in Everywoman* did for women by providing images and descriptions of the archetypes within men, and in this case, within women as well. It is becoming an influence in the growing Men's Movement.

In 1990, *Goddesses in Everywoman* is still in print, and seems more available in bookstores than when it was first published. After six years, I can see the influence it has had, and appreciate that one of its most important contributions is to women's spirituality. The book was about women's psychology, but it gave a vocabulary to women, empowering them to further define their own psychological experience, which, at a deep level, is spiritual. Recalling that "psychology" comes from the Greek word, *psyche*, which means "soul," this is as it should be.

Each of the archetypes has a sacred dimension. For example, a woman who is deeply maternal responds as Demeter; when she nurses her child and is fully present and undistracted, she may feel herself enacting a sacrament. Lovemaking is imbued with beauty and love, and made sacred when the archetype of Aphrodite in her temple is present in the moment. Housecleaning that is done with the inner mediative consciousness of Hestia is a centering experience. An Artemis is on sacred ground out in nature.

As women came to consciously know and honor the archetypes that were active within themselves, they were attending to the symbolic level of the psyche, which contributed to the creation of private sacred places; an altar space on a table top, a meditation room, a place in a garden or out in nature, places where symbolic objects that reflected a woman's inner depth were placed, honoring the goddess within the woman. No outside authority or extrinsic worth determined what would be a "sacred object" or what constituted an "altar space."

Goddesses in Everywoman was one of many books that nourished a grassroots womens' spirituality movement — contributing to, or coinciding with profound inner phenomenological experiences of the goddess. Goddess figures began appearing in women's dreams, in active imagination, in psychic or mystic states (noted throughout 1980, but with increasing frequency toward the end of the decade). Experiences of the goddess, in turn, inspired art, poetry, music and literature.

There is something awesome or numinous that makes a figure a "goddess." It is a subjective experience that is truly consciousness-raising: to have an experience of divinity as female, of god as a woman goes against the fundamental teaching of all patriarchal theologies in which men, not women, are created in the image of God. Patriarchal religion gives men dominion over women, children, and nature, and this in turn contributes to dysfunctional families, societies, and to a potential nuclear or ecological disaster. For power over others leads too easily to abuse of power, and to aggressive competition for power.

The sacred, spiritual, theological dimension of women's experience has a central place in women's psyches. A woman who is empowered trusts the authenticity of her own experience. A slogan of feminism has been "the personal is political"; once we get into the practice of defining ourselves, which is a goal of good psychotherapy, we find *the personal is also spiritual*. It seems to me, for the individual woman and for the planet, that women's spirituality is the last and most significant wave of the women's movement.

It has been a rewarding journey, to go from being a silent psychiatric resident who did not ask why women were defined by the penis we lacked instead of what we did have, to being the author of *Goddesses in Everywoman*. Along the way, I learned that the feminist perspective, is at heart, deeply personal. Outer authority and expert opinion have no jurisdiction, when the authenticity of our own lived experience is the source of our knowledge.

REFERENCES

Bolen, J. S. (1984). *Goddesses in Everywoman*. San Francisco: Harper & Row.
Bolen, J. S. (1989). *Gods in Everyman*. San Francisco: Harper & Row.
Claremont de Castillejo, I (1973). *Knowing Woman*. New York: Putnam's Sons.
Deutsch, Helene. (1944). *Psychology of Women*. Grune & Stratton.
Friedan, B. (1964). *The Feminine Mystique*. New York: Dell.
Harding, M. E. (1933). *The Way of All Women*. New York: Putnam's.
Heilbrun, C. G. (1979). *Reinventing Womanhood*. New York: Norton.
Henning, M. & Jardin, A. (1978). *The Managerial Woman*. New York: Simon & Schuster.
Jung, E. (1969). *Animus and Anima*. New York: Spring.
Jung, C. G. (1968). Archetypes of the Collective Unconscious. *Collected Works of C. G. Jung, 9*. Part 1.
Jung, C. G. Psychological types (1971). *Collected works of C.G. Jung, 6*.
Miller, J. B. (1973). *Psychoanalysis and Women*. New York: Brunner/Mazel.
Neumann, E. (1956). *Amor and Psyche: The psychic development of the feminine*. Translated by Ralph Manheim. Bollingen Series 54. New York: Pantheon Books.
Seidenberg, R. (1973). The Trauma of Eventlessness. In J. B. Miller (ed.) *Psychoanalysis and Women*. Baltimore: Penguin.
Shulman, A. K. (1972). *Memoirs of an Ex-Prom Queen*. New York: Knopf.

My Personal Education as a Feminist Therapist

Judith J. Frankel

There was no training for me as a feminist therapist. My exposure to explicitly feminist research or theory was limited to a chance conversation on the telephone with a fellow graduate student. This discussion was an attempt to guess what questions might be asked on the second section of our doctoral preliminary examinations the next morning, one day in April of 1971. She happened to mention that one of her professors had recently noted Matina Horner's new research and she thought that it might appear as a topic on prelims. Indeed it did. With this one exception, there was no study or discussion in any of my graduate classes of any feminist issues or research.

Yet, I was — am — naturally feminist in my thinking, my therapy, my approach to life. Feminism is as natural as breathing; equality is a given, not a privilege. It never occurred to me as a child, for example, that I could be prevented from doing or becoming whatever I wished to be professionally. I credit my mother, especially, for that sense of boundless personal development.

At an early age, I decided to focus on psychology. Later, a crush on my professor for Introductory Psychology, a handsome as well as bright man, gave further impetus to my decision. The clincher,

---

Judith J. Frankel, PhD, is a Clinical and Consulting Psychologist in private practice, her role for the past 14 years. During the same period, she was on the faculty at Pennsylvania State University, gave birth to her two daughters, wrote a book, and became a single-parent-head-of-household. Common to those of us in the sandwich generation, she also assumed additional responsibilities for her aging mother.

© 1991 by The Haworth Press, Inc. All rights reserved.

however, was the excitement I experienced in studying with an exceptionally intelligent young woman psychology professor.

I received quality graduate training in psychology, but it was the standard fare and exposed me to virtually no theory, research or clinical skills of relevance to feminist therapy. I have since read feminist books and research articles, held discussions, taught classes, and conducted therapy as a feminist. Indeed, I have even carried my convictions into my synagogue, joining because the Reconstructionist movement in Judaism embraces equality and empowerment of women in the life of the congregation as well as in its philosophy of life.

Never have I, however, experienced a supportive formal professional context for my feminist interests in either therapy or teaching. I was in graduate school at a time which preceded the development of courses on psychology of women or the acknowledgement of the importance of feminist perspectives in therapy. In my professional life, there was no forum for discussing how the, at the time, new feminist insights would inform the work of myself and my colleagues. We were too early for women's studies programs, feminist therapist associations, or sessions of the American Psychological Association devoted to feminist psychology. In a very real sense, my inner feminist beliefs were finding a voice in my professional activities as the Women's Movement was finding its voice.

Ironically, during my second job interview as a new Ph.D., I was likened to Bella Abzug by the highest level administrator who interviewed me. Ms. Abzug was raising her voice loudly at that time in the political arena as a liberal and as a feminist. The analogy was not meant as a compliment; I did not get the job.

The position I was offered, as director of program development and evaluation for a primary prevention center funded on soft money, had its own pitfalls for an unwary and naive feminist. The university department in which my appointment was located had only one other woman faculty member at that time. She was three decades older than I, and she was continually ridiculed by her male colleagues when she was not being ignored. My recollections of faculty meetings are that this professor spoke rarely, and when she did speak, she made a joke of what she was saying as though she could not take herself seriously either. Yet, embedded within those jokes were always significant points, if only they could be heard. I remember feeling impatient with my colleagues for not hearing her voice, for refusing to hear her meaning. I also remember feeling impatient with her for not being more direct. However, as the most junior assistant professor and as a woman, I was in a weak position to redirect that group.

I later came to realize two things. First, my female colleague was wise: she had long ago discerned that she would not be listened to by those men, so she developed a jocular and somewhat apologetic strategy for bringing some attention her way. Second, she and I were both completely excluded from the very active old-boy network in the department itself. All the young-boy colleagues were included, but the club allowed no women. She, as I, had had to make her way alone.

My exclusion from this old-boy network had many ramifications. Among them was an unfortunate clustering of factors that led to an interesting but extremely difficult experience with a graduate level class I taught my first year. When I was hired for the position, I was told that I would be expected to teach one graduate class and I was asked which course I would like to teach. After examining the course offerings, I selected one on counseling methodologies. The department head told me to go ahead with it, casually mentioning that one of the faculty members might have some notes he could share with me for preparing the course. I began to teach in the spring term. From the beginning, it was a challenge and it progressed to a disaster. The most obvious factor was that the text I had selected, a new one, had been ordered but was not received by the bookstore until well into mid-semester. Other factors emerged as more important issues. The one I discovered first was that the majority of the graduate students in the class had just begun in graduate school that very term. I had prepared the course on the assumption that these students already had two terms under their belts and therefore were not only oriented to the program, but also knowledgeable about basic concepts. I realized much later that I had had no way of knowing that any other possibility existed: I had never been given an orientation to the program myself. It is my belief that had I been a man, I would have been given basic information by the department head; at least my fellow male colleagues would have taken me aside and told me what I needed to know.

My second major discovery came almost at the end of the course, when an active rebellion rocked the class. A concerned student asked to see me, and this student informed me that many of the others had been incited to riot by another faculty member who was livid that I had been given "his" course to teach. As it turned out, this faculty member, my "colleague," had been leading many of the students in direct sabotage of my class all term long. A number of the new graduate students had been assigned to this particular faculty member as advisees, and he had taken it upon himself to tell them just how he would teach the course and what a bad job I was doing. Again, I attribute some of the difficulties I experienced not only to this vitriolic colleague's egomania, but to the old boys who failed to inform me of some important realities. Years later, I heard from several students in that class how much they had learned from me; indeed, they have all gone on to become prominent in their areas. And most are women, so I am doubly delighted.

There was yet another way in which I discovered I did not belong to the old-boy network. I was responsible for conceptualizing, designing, implementing (with my staff), analyzing, interpreting, and writing up major research projects as well as primary prevention programs themselves. My immediate boss, the man who had received the grant to fund this center, made it clear that he expected to be included as author on all publications. I refused. I told him that I believed that such an expectation was directly contrary to the ethics of the profession, and I asserted that I would not act counter to those ethics. I did not view such an assertion then as a feminist assertion. Later, I came to realize that it was indeed, for the operations of the old-boy network often relied upon the "you scratch my back, I'll scratch yours" mentality. Through my refusal to conform to this model, I set myself up as a non-cooperator, not a "team player," and for this I was never forgiven. Thereafter, I remained even more isolated and cut out of the power structure. The lack of support was palpable, as was the envy for the praise I received for the development and research work I was doing.

More often than not, I found myself teased or ridiculed for my feminist positions. Early on, I shocked my boss, my fellow faculty member, when I confronted him about his asking his secretary to pour his coffee. I suggested to him that while her job description included many responsibilities, pouring coffee for others was not one of them. He was taken aback by this assertion, not said in a hostile way, but he continued to call his secretary to pour his coffee. Thereafter, however, he ridiculed me in front of others for my stance.

Others teased me for my gender-neutral language in the classroom and in my writing; I always used and continue to use such language in therapy. Remarks were commonly addressed to me about the awkwardness of "s/he" or "she or he" when "they" would not be appropriate to use. One male colleague with whom I was struggling to write a book constantly made fun of my attempts to be non-sexist. This was the same colleague who had contracted to write one-third of our book and who ultimately wrote no more than several sentences, all from the original prospectus. When I asserted that his input was less than equitable, he made insulting remarks to me. The most insulting, and the one I will never forget, was "Heil Hitler."

I made it a point always to use gender-neutral language in the classroom and in therapy, and it became an informal study for me to trace the rising consciousness of my students and my clients in their spoken and written language. I would like to think that I influenced many people to be aware of their language and its implications and to be non-sexist in their approach to living. I do know that by the end of each course, most students were using gender-neutral language in the classroom. With clients, the possibility and necessity of examining sexism and its impact on their inner lives and their relationships at home and at work extended the impact of the language I used in our sessions.

My own research and therapeutic endeavors have had as a metaframework the search for those mechanisms that promote equality, particularly between partners in intimate relationships. Exploring decision-making about sexual behavior in heterosexual relationships, I examined moral reasoning, sexual philosophy, and interpersonal interaction as central variables to discern approaches to decision-making. Among other intriguing outcomes, it was apparent that some women and men spontaneously establish egalitarian relationships with feminist/humanist values as well as observable shared power. This was seen in how they reasoned about "right" and "wrong" and in their articulation and implementation of democratic processes in their interactions.

Findings relevant to this observation led to my paper on "Personal Freedom in Intimate Interpersonal Relationships" (D'Augelli-Frankel, 1974) which in turn suggested an approach to understanding relationship dynamics which has been termed "relationship reasoning." Theoretically parallel to moral reasoning as advanced by Lawrence Kohlberg, relationship reasoning is conceptualized to be developmental in process and to potentially evolve to a level in which what is valued are the ethics of reciprocity and mutuality in a context of equal, shared power. Several new pieces of writing and new approaches to therapeutic practice became outgrowths of this as well. At the therapy level I explored the concept in chapters on sex therapy and at the therapist level in an article entitled, "Some of my Best Friends are Sexist: An Essay in Therapist Self-exploration" (D'Augelli-Frankel, 1982).

Of course what is valued is not always consistently enacted and is often obstructed in its enactment. As a feminist therapist concerned with egalitarianism, empowerment, relationship reciprocity, relationship connection, and identity achievement free from sexist distortions, I have found myself challenged by and challenging this truism.

As a feminist therapist, I attempt to nourish the strengths, talents, and inner resources of each client just as I attempt to nourish each client's sense of connection and relationship with significant people in her or his life. As a feminist therapist, I attempt to help each client find ways of nourishing self and relationships for her- or himself and ways of understanding how to develop and enhance egalitarian relationships in both personal and professional contexts. Perhaps Carol Gilligan (1982) best describes my own thinking about this:

> The reinterpretation of women's experience in terms of their own imagery of relationships thus clarifies that experience and also provides a nonhierarchial vision of human connection. Since relationships, when cast in the image of hierarchy, ap-

pear inherently unstable and morally problematic, their transposition into the image of web changes an order of inequality into a structure of interconnection. But the power of the images of hierarchy and web, their evocation of feelings and their recurrence in thought, signifies the embeddedness of both these images in the cycle of human life. The experiences of inequality and interconnection, inherent in the relation of parent and child, then give rise to the ethics of justice and care, the ideals of human relationship—the vision that self and other will be treated as of equal worth, that despite differences in power, things will be fair; the vision that everyone will be responded to and included, that no one will be left alone or hurt. These disparate visions in their tension reflect the paradoxical truths of human experience—that we know ourselves as separate only insofar as we live in connection with others, and that we experience relationship only insofar as we differentiate other from self. (pp. 62-63)

Rabbi Hillel, many centuries ago, expressed a similar notion: "If I am not for myself, who will be for me? If I am only for myself, what kind of person am I? And if not now, when?"

As a therapist committed to feminist/humanist values and their implementation in living, I have tried to bring the lessons from my own life into my understanding of the needs, relationships, and lives of others. My life experience has been, in part, my training or at least the catalyst for my intuitive and focused orientation to the experiences and issues of those with whom I work in therapy in ways that often were not spoken about, much less taught, during my graduate school career.

In fact, there are many aspects of women's life needs in which I had had no training or background before entering professional practice. Referrals often introduced me as a young therapist to issues and experiences I had not otherwise been introduced to at all. One early example was the referral by an obstetrician of a young woman who had had a miscarriage months earlier, but who remained seriously depressed. In exploring the depression, it became clear that she was mourning the loss of her child; she was overwhelmed by grief. The miscarriage had been in the first trimester, but she had formed a bond with this unborn child that was exceptionally strong and very real. No readings, courses, practica, or even informal discussions in graduate school had raised miscarriage as a possible, potential or even likely source of emotional pain, much less depression. As time went on, I discovered that this was not an isolated occurrence; a number of women were referred or referred themselves for this same reason. I later had a miscarriage of my own and learned firsthand some of the power of carrying life within oneself — and losing it.

My experiences in therapy, research, academia, marriage, divorce, parenting and the single life have been rich and varied. There have been professional and personal issues and dilemmas throughout, including the interesting experience of attempting to "practice what I preach." Theorizing is easy; implementation is more difficult and far more complicated. I have been fortunate to develop, over time, a network of feminist colleagues and friends who support each other and who pursue the "repair of the world" through professional activity in feminist therapy, research, teaching, and activism. I am still learning, as a woman who is a feminist as well as a feminist who is a therapist.

REFERENCES

D'Augelli-Frankel, J. (1974). Personal freedom in intimate interpersonal relationships. Paper presented at the annual meeting of the National Council on Family Relations, Toronto, Canada, October 1973, and published in Packet A: *Pluralism in Family Styles*. Minneapolis, Minn: NCFR Edu-Tapes.

D'Augelli-Frankel, J. (1982). Some of my best friends are sexist: An essay in therapist self-exploration. In P. Keller and L. Ritt (Eds.). *Innovations in Clinical Practice*: A Sourcebook. Sarasota, FL: Professional Resource Exchange.

Gilligan, C. (1982). *In a Different Voice*. Cambridge, Mass.: Harvard University Press.

Thinking Together

Michele Clark

The following incident highlights, for me, how the women's movement came directly out of the anti-war movement. It is the winter of 1969, I am twenty-three years old and I am standing in the office in which I work, Liberation News Service (LNS), and I am crying. I don't know why I'm crying but it has something to do with ways I feel I should be acting like a tough revolutionary, but really I want a boyfriend and I miss my mother. As I cry I talk to a male friend of mine, another LNS writer. A woman our age from the adjacent office of Students for a Democratic Society, stops in the doorway, and asks "What are you two talking about so intensely?"

My friend answers, "Oh, you know, our problems."

She frowns, exasperated, "Oh you two," she says, "You're *always* talking about your problems."

Within the year this woman disappeared into the Weatherman Underground, the man moved to New York and came out as a homosexual and I was living in Cambridge, Massachusetts, a member of Collective Number One of Bread and Roses.

Bread and Roses was a short-lived, dynamic, anarchic, feminist organization founded by women who had been active in the student anti-war movement. It was created, in part, in response to the bullying posture which had become standard in the New Left, the Weather Underground being the extreme example; and, in part, in response to new ideas about women. Collective Number One was a consciousness raising group of eight women within Bread and

---

Michele Clark, MEd, is living in Plainfield, VT on an extended leave from the Women's Mental Health Collective. She is not yet sure if clinical life outside a women's collective is possible. She recently completed a research paper on education groups for adult daughters of alcoholics, and is teaching in the Adult Degree Option at Lesley College.

Roses. We met once a week to take about our doubts, angers, fears and what we observed as typical interactions between men and women. We would then use these feelings and observations, along with reading and writing, to make a political, social analysis.

It was, for me, the beginning of learning to be both a feminist and a therapist. We were trying to talk honestly about what we experienced and rename it (the therapist part) and we were trying to use this talk to analyze social structure and social attitudes (the feminist part). Among the many activities which Bread and Roses sponsored were public, sample consciousness-raising groups. In these, we would offer other women an opportunity to talk about their lives and listen to us talk about the insights and sense of transformation we were experiencing. Women would enter these open groups curious, but defended. "I don't have these problems. . . . My boyfriend and I get along great . . . we never fight . . . My parents never treated me differently from my brother . . ." It seemed to take about six meetings for a woman to get it. At that point she might form her own ongoing consciousness-raising group, join Bread and Roses, or do whatever was the next step for her. This was a heady and exhilarating time. The student anti-war movement was both the frame of reference we were rebelling against, and also the frame of reference in which we had developed our basic analysis. We were both part of the movement and leaving it behind.

I did not have a professional identity at this time, and I was conflicted about whether or not I wanted one. I had worked only in "movement" jobs — on the underground press or doing street theater. This was, in part, because of my ideals, in part because I was afraid of the world of work and unprepared for it. I was a puzzle to myself and my family which was a large, close, extended Jewish family in New York City. It was unusual for anyone in my family to go out of town to college, and even rarer for anyone, after college, to move away from the metropolitan area. I had spent the year after college traveling around the country and had ended up living in Cambridge for, from my family's point of view, no good reason.

My parents were ambivalent about whether or not I needed to support myself. They would have been relieved and pleased to see me married and a mother. I was confused about these things as well. Not only was I the first female in my family to live an uncharted life, I was the first person of either gender.

So I spent hours talking with my friends about what I vaguely called my problems—which, to sum up now, were an extended bout of guilt and separation anxiety. I read the kind of semi-popular psychology books which came my way—Rollo May, Erich Fromm, Fritz Perls, Paul Goodman, Carl Rogers—whatever was around at that time. None of these men really addressed what I was going through. However, they made the idea and style of psychotherapy familiar.

Later, in 1976, when I was in the Women's Mental Health Collective, we compiled statistics about our clients and discovered that many of the young women who came to us for therapy were, like me, the first female child who could choose options other than marriage and motherhood; a pioneer in role expectations. We used this as a theme to help young women understand their personal difficulties in a larger framework. This was one of our first conceptualizations which explained, without blaming the mother, why it was hard for the daughter to do what she was doing. It put the daughter, who was our client, and her problem in a social context. At the same time it acknowledged that being a pioneer was difficult and frightening; that a woman might need help.

After Bread and Roses dissolved I was mentored by a woman who had just finished her residency in psychiatry. She offered me a job team-teaching a course with her on the psychology of women, really a consciousness-raising course combined with academic reading. "Mentored" is not the word this woman and I used for our relationship. We were, and are, good friends. We spent a good deal of time talking about men, women, books, films, people, and ideas. But, in retrospect, I see that this was a mentoring relationship in that she could see I was good at something, she encouraged me to keep at it and offered me an opportunity to grow in competence. She had a clear professional identity which I didn't have. Our course was a great success. My friend and my then boyfriend, now husband, both began to urge me to go back to school and get a degree in mental health work.

The Masters program in counseling that I entered was designed for adults. The youngest student was twenty-five and most people had several years of front-line mental health experience working with delinquent teenagers, disturbed children and others in state social service settings. I was the least experienced, but I was the most politically sophisticated and feminist person in the program. For example, when one of the teachers in a course on society and psychology said that society isn't run for the benefit of all, there was a class gasp of shock. But I already knew this. That year, in Boston, there was a horrible murder. Several Black teenage boys doused a White woman with kerosene and set her on fire. This crime was discussed in class and in the newspapers as a problem of race relations or a problem of violence in our society. I was the one who raised the issue, in the classroom, of this being a problem of violence against women. After some of these discussions other students would come up to me and say things like, "I always get so much out of what you say." This kind of dialogue and appreciation was good for me, it helped me place myself in the larger world as a competent person.

My practicum supervisor was a psychoanalytically oriented psychologist; really, I think, a rather nice man, interested in transference, yet condemned to work half-time in a community mental health center where one rarely got to issues of transference. He wanted to assign the chronic mental patients to the M.A. and M.Ed students, and save the healthier clients for the psychology and psychiatry interns. We fought over this and each won a little. I saw some people with chronic major mental illness and he assigned me three people with relatively mild problems in living.

In this practicum, which was only nine months long, I learned that what I was doing, what you do when you do therapy is *form an alliance*. Now, in a sense, I had been forming alliances all my life. This is what women do well, isn't it? So this was nothing new. At the same time it was naming and recognizing a skill I had, but had never named. I also learned that, contrary to what Fritz Perls implied, therapy is not about letting it all hang out, but, on the contrary, about keeping it together. These were both very valuable lessons.

After I received my degree I worked for a year in a chronic ward of a state hospital. This gave me a feel for the range of mental illness and for how the system did or didn't operate.

THE WOMEN'S MENTAL HEALTH COLLECTIVE

In 1975 I was invited to join the Women's Mental Health Collective (WMHC). The group had been together five years. Its five members had all, like me, been active in anti-war and then feminist organizations. At present, 1990, the Women's Mental Health Collective is a free-standing, licensed clinic in Somerville, Massachusetts.

Although I was not involved in the earliest years, I have heard these stories so often that they have become my own, like family history.

The WMHC first came together as a support group for feminist women finishing their graduate studies in psychiatry, psychology, social work and counseling. Graduate school had been, in part, an education in power differentials—clients humiliated at grand rounds, a woman student given a hard time by her thesis advisor because he didn't think women should be in graduate school, a woman patient given a punitive diagnosis because she didn't use charm with the doctor. Case conferences often consisted of rote mother-blaming.

The Collective first offered psychotherapy within a free clinic, and later became autonomous. The Collective had a secret name which was *Friends of Dora*. This was in recognition of the fact that, even without an analysis of sexual abuse, in simply reading about the case of Dora, a feminist could see that Freud had skewed his diagnosis and treatment in order to protect Dora's uncle and father. Much later, two collective members, Judith Herman and Emily Schatzow, were pioneers in treating and writing about father-daughter incest. This early, private joke was a prescient recognition of ways psychology had been used against women, prescient of all the re-naming of women we were about to discover.

In the beginning of the Collective, when members had at most one year of clinical experience, we would see individual clients in pairs. This seems comical now, but it served several useful functions. It helped the anxiety level of the new clinician, and also mitigated against mistakes. It built group solidarity and helped Collective members see that while their theoretical training was different, their practice was similar. Now, of course, we see individual clients individually. However, collective members continue to write papers and create and run groups in pairs. Pairing is both a way to learn by talk and feedback, and is more stimulating than working alone. Also, it's more fun.

At the point that I joined the Collective we began a series of biweekly meetings to talk about our mothers and share data on our clients. We were groping toward what one would now call positive reframing. We knew women were treated badly in the mental health system and we knew women's strengths were used against them, but exactly what these strengths were and how to do it differently, we were still trying to find out. Our mothers, we all felt, had been hopelessly inadequate in equipping us for the modern world, but we could see that putting the blame on them had only limited utility and, eventually, would rebound on us as women and mothers.

As we talked about our mothers we began to see that, given their personal circumstances and the historical time, they had each attempted to stretch their own limits. As one woman talked about her mother, another would say something admiring or appreciative. In this way we discovered that each of our mothers really was worthy of admiration and appreciation; she didn't sound so bad to someone else. This was illuminating information. Among other things, these meetings made us understand that the royal road to self-esteem in women lay, not only in faulting the mother, but, as often, in appreciating her.

My own growth and our development as a group has always been in dialogue with other women in the field. During the time we were conducting our mother-daughter investigations, Jean Baker Miller was writing her book *The Psychology of Women* (1976) and giving talks about her ideas. We went to hear her speak and also met with her a few times at our office. Her ideas about how women's combined injunction and capacity to nurture is both demanded and discredited, helped us articulate our own observations and ideas. Similarly, in 1980 we attended two conferences with the *Women's Project in Family Therapy*. These conferences also helped us clarify a critique we were already developing about the nature of separation and individuation within the family. The most important thing we learned is that separation is rarely complete and complete separation is rarely desirable. We also learned to observe and work with the process as well as the content in both family and individual therapy.

Doris Lessing once remarked that she no longer considered that she had a thought, but, rather, that there was a thought around. My experience of the women's movement and the development of a feminist approach to psychotherapy has been the experience of being an individual within a much larger group of women in which we are, each, observing, thinking, feeling, speaking, listening, and writing — in that order — and then we do it over again, together.

From Black Person to Black Female to African-American Woman: A Critical Developmental Transition for a Feminist Therapist

Robbie J. Steward

INTRODUCTION

Black Person

Once upon a time, seemingly very long ago, I was a star. Everything that I touched seemed to shine with the glow of success and hope. My family of origin was supportive of my personal as well as my professional goals. My working class Black community in a small rural town in southwestern Oklahoma was encouraging, always acknowledging my accomplishments. The racially integrated school system consistently offered me opportunities to excel, guidance in career decision-making, and validation for efforts that set me apart personally and academically from many of my peers, both Black and White. I was certainly blessed, which allowed me the innocence of thinking that I was in full control of all of these events. I sincerely believed that I received what I did because I deserved it and because the world was fair and just. I knew of the Civil Rights

---

Robbie J. Steward began her doctoral training in Counseling Psychology at the University of Oklahoma in 1979 and completed the requirements in 1984. As Assistant Professor in the University of Kansas Department of Counseling Psychology, her professional/research interests include the following: cross-cultural counseling; women's issues and career satisfaction in the academic environment; professional impairment in the mental health profession; and racial/ethnic minority student academic success. She has been married for 15 years and is the mother of a five-year-old daughter.

© 1991 by The Haworth Press, Inc. All rights reserved.

Movement, but had no framework upon which to conceptualize what was actually happening in the world of other persons who suffered oppression. I engaged with Whites and Blacks quite successfully, and felt so powerful and in control. My loyalty was to my people for it was among them that I felt the strongest support, but I had not an inkling of what the struggle of my people was. I was a Black person, in fact, a person who just happened to be Black. I was a star . . . a bright, shining, innocent.

Black Female

I was able to maintain the delusion of the just world for many, many years. I received both bachelor's and master's degrees without changing my perception of myself nor that of the world. In fact, my delusion was strongly reinforced by the predominantly White world in which I existed. I was special and was told in many not so subtle ways that I was more special than any of the other Blacks. By this I was thoroughly confused because all of the Black people I knew were special, but in my mind had chosen another path. (What else could I think, since I believed that everyone was truly in control of their world!) I was also quite curious by this message from the White world, because I felt that I was much brighter than many of their own, but to these individuals, I was never compared. It is not that during this period of innocence I did not have any experiences that could easily have been interpreted as racist or sexist, but that the only framework I had to explain them was to attribute such to coincidence or personality differences.

For example, during my junior year in zoology a professor accused me of stealing my collection of invertebrates which was required for the course. He blatantly told me in a tiny room with an assistant, that I had stolen the specimens from the lab downstairs. I was wounded! I would have died before stealing anything, given my very Black Southern Baptist background. I cried and cried, and felt powerless. Much of my collection had in fact come from supporters in my small city of origin. We were told that we could access any resource possible and I happened to have had connections with veterinarians and physicians who had what I needed. After the accusation, my supporters did write in my defense, but a major transition had occurred that felt devastating, but would lead me on toward a new awareness of the world. I now had some idea that the world was not always fair and that I was not always in control even when I was doing my best. I could no longer go to class. The professor would not acknowledge my upraised hand to answer questions. I tried so hard to continue in spite of his behaviors toward me. I could not . . . did not. I felt wounded. I received an F. I was challenged to seek legal counsel, but it was against my values to rock the boat, so I did not. No class could have offered me this insight by reading a text. These feelings were new and frightening, but as with many new and frightening feelings and insights, were put aside for me to pursue a goal of which I had never lost sight: the doctoral degree. My family and community offered full support. Repression became my defense of choice, but other subtle and consistent messages, of which I was not always aware, were being relayed and were slowly wearing to a frazzle my delusion of control and fairness. I was still a star, not shining as brightly, but beginning to feel as if I had hard work to do to prove that I was a shining star to those who had a hard time seeing what I knew was there, what my family and community had told me was there. I wanted these strangers to know that I was special too . . . that they know was so important, too important. What I had done naturally and felt naturally in terms of self-efficacy, self-concept and self-worth was now something I had to prove. I was becoming a Black female, a statistic.

Being a Black female for me was wrought with anxiety and obsessive-compulsive behaviors. My graduate student peers were friendly. I had faculty support. So, I was not alone, but I did have some sense that I was less than, or different, or at least perceived differently. This vague sense of alienation was first validated in a Multicultural course which examined the societal beliefs and reactions to women and racial/ethnic minorities. The following is an excerpt from a log I wrote for the instructor following the first few class periods.

"Before the second class meeting, I had falsely assumed that Multicultural Counseling would be a 'fun' class. This fallacy in thought was perpetuated by the innocuous material covered during the first class meeting. I felt very comfortable in my (all White) subgroup discussing the goals of counseling and how those related to what we actually perceive an emotionally healthy person to be. I actively participated in presenting my views and accepted all positive feedback. All of my contributions had been integrated into the group's overall decision and I felt that I had attained a goal that is very important to me . . . acceptance. I felt good after class and left very excited about what was to come. My blissful world of ignorance and peace ended here, being totally replaced with confusion, anger, and knowledge. 'Which state was better?' I continue to ask myself. I don't know, but I have no choice now, I can only go forward."

"The discomfort started during the second session when the film about racial issues in the classroom was shown. I felt something, but initially I could not identify it. It was only after the discussion of the film that it dawned on me. Everyone started to give their individual observations, assumptions, and evaluations of the film. That was when it jarred me, I was different because I had emotional reactions to the movie and had not only observed. Then it shook me, no, it swept through me like a freezing wind and settled there. Everyone (except three others who for some reason I couldn't see) was White and I was Black . . . am Black . . . had always been . . . and that was perceived as bad by many. I didn't want to look . . . I didn't want to look at them, but I had to see and hear and it hurt. The idea that people with whom I spent most of my time were racist made me suddenly feel isolated and defensive. Hurriedly I left class, alone."

"Coming back was very difficult and I didn't want to. I did not want to hear others' blatant ignorance and I definitely did not feel responsible for their reeducation. So once I found I had no alternative, I prayed and prayed and prayed. Initially I prayed for God to take me up because I couldn't stand it anymore. He didn't. Next I prayed that my anger and intolerance and hurt would dissipate and be replaced with patience and understanding. He answered. Thank God for that because the next meeting I was to role-play an angry

White male student. It was difficult the first few moments, but became easier and easier . . . I felt so White, right, and misunderstood, and yet so powerful. I learned and understood."

During this period, I pleaded with the instructor (a wonderful, very competent, well-known Jewish woman in the field of Multicultural Counseling) to allow me to drop this class. My argument was that I could not deal with the content and exist in this class. She smiled, gave me a hug and validation, but would not allow it. The following day she and her assistant left a poster for me that said, "The truth will set you free, but first it will make you very miserable!" The poster had a Raggedy Ann doll moving through a wringer on an old model washing machine. It was perfect and very appropriate, for that was what I had been: a "pretty doll" that had been on the shelf. Now on my way to the real world, in the trenches, I had to go through the wringer to understand and be of some assistance to my people of color, to my sisters in the struggle, and to those of Anglo origin who had an interest in changing social norms that were toxic to my own. I was now on my way to becoming an African-American woman, who is not only defined by skin color, but by a heritage that has legitimate roots, history, and strength.

African-American Woman

Being an African-American woman in my experience is being aware of all aspects of self and the influence of those parts upon those around you. I can feel and validate those feelings through expression. I can behave in more ways than a Black female would ever conceive. I can be challenging and challenged without the fear of being vulnerable, for I am strong, not tough, having something to prove as the Black female, but strong, having been through the wringer of awareness and knowing that my personal power and strength go to the very core of my soul. Being a Black female was being angry at people for wanting to take away my power and status, while being an African-American woman is being curious and somewhat amused that any people or person would believe that they actually could. Being an African-American woman is willing to be aggressive, not just assertive, but actively changing and questioning what should not be. Though I have not yet fully self-actualized, I did recognize when I had truly made a positive transition into the world of African-American women.

During my doctoral internship I was once again the only Black among the interns. Having grown comfortable with expressing my perceptions and views, at times I felt once again as if I was a person who happened to be Black. I felt powerful in that not only could I effectively deal with content, but also was able to rely on and value my intuition as well. My supervisors were consistently pleased with my performance overall. However, I did have one dilemma. At times, my peers were not quite able to hear what I was saying. It would seem that I would speak, but no one would acknowledge what I had said, and then sometime later someone else in the group would say the same thing and receive acknowledgement and validation for coming up with such a critical observation or suggestion. I allowed this to happen several times, just to check for continuity of a pattern. When I brought this observation to the group supervisor and group members, the recommendation was that my timing might have been a little off and that I might observe what others were doing. This suggestion felt familiar in that I had been told to watch the effectiveness of others, particularly during my Black female stage. I did watch, and what I saw was that not only was my timing similar, but when I spoke there were some group members who did not even acknowledge my presence with eye contact. It was further interesting that these members were male and very powerful within the group. I was alone. No one validated my observations or my willingness to share them. Assertion does not always work, and I knew this by now. However, I had also learned to give people the benefit of the doubt in their ability to see through personal blindspots. They did not. I waited for the perfect moment when a few members of the group were doing a fishbowl exercise where we were being observed by the other five interns. The same dynamic occurred. I was not spoken to and eye contact was maintained between the two men. When I spoke, nonverbals of dismissal were received. I did not process the dynamic. I did not express hurt or disappointment because of their inability to hear and/or see me. I picked up my chair and, before everyone, moved me and it to a position where both men could not overlook my presence. From then on I received both acknowledgement and eye contact. No words were spoken about what I had done for there was no need. I remain on good terms with all group members, which few others in the group could say. I harbor no bad feelings, for I did what was necessary: value me as I respect and value others. I am now an African-American woman!

THE IMPACT UPON MY ROLE AS THERAPIST

The Multicultural course was certainly a critical event in my professional and personal development. The content allowed me to conceptualize my experience as well as that of others, including clients, very differently. The impact of environment and societal reactions to particular groups and gender issues can at times be overwhelming. So overwhelming that failure can result as it did for me in my invertebrate course. The belief in a just and fair world was shattered and I had to review experiences where I had done everything I knew possible (within my value system) to attain acceptance and/or validation and failed. I was able to understand my clients' dilemmas at a deeper level and have increased empathy for all issues and presenting problems. The underlining impetus for all of my behaviors during the development of the therapeutic relationship has become the empowerment of clients and I am willing to adopt the advocacy role when appropriate. I am also more aware of the importance of the development and maintenance of a fully functioning support network of persons who are sensitive to issues which must be overcome. I now know that the individualistic, competitive system that is set as the norm is not and should not be functional for all as long as society perpetuates the valuing of one group over another. I have learned from wonderful female role models of varying interpersonal styles that flexibility and at times militancy are truly the keys to survival for all of us.

SUMMARY

The transition from Black Person, to Black Female, to African-American Woman was very critical for me in both my professional and personal development. I am frightened that I might have lived my life as only a person who happened to be Black and missed out on the peace, sense of self-validation, and acceptance of others as they are which has resulted from the painful experience of moving toward the African-American Woman. I have learned to have increased respect for other women who have gone through the trenches during a period when femaleness was even more so equated with meaninglessness than today. I now truly honor and hold in greater esteem those African-American women who thrived and excelled in environments that perceived my people as only animals, less than human. I owe these women the commitment to continue toward the reeducation of our current society, not only of tolerance of females, but the acceptance and value of the uniqueness our presence offers. This I will do for I am, we are, stars: bright, shining, and knowledgeable. We owe it to our sisters and brothers to shine so that all might see.

Courage in the Trenches

Toni Napoli

I am a feminist therapist. Feminist therapy simply means believing, understanding, and empowering women. My feminist views, theories, and training evolved from the experiences of trauma in my life. This evolution occurred during the 1960s and 1970s, a time of turbulence and change. I was involved in the women's movement working for women's causes. Basically, my feminist professional training was received in the trenches, where courageous therapists were already working with women's issues such as domestic abuse and sexual assault. Unfortunately, my story of trauma is not unique. Millions of women have the same or similar story. Fortunately, women have banded together to change the stories of our lives.

It all began in Seattle, Washington, on an October day in 1969. I was 25 years old, had been married a year, and was very happily pregnant with our first child. I had recently cut back my work hours and was enjoying a Monday at home cleaning the house. At 11:00 that morning the trauma of my life was about to unfold as a neatly dressed young man came to our door. He asked to use the telephone and I responded with a firm "no." I proceeded to shut the door, whereupon he proved to be stronger than I and pushed his way in. With quite a struggle, he proceeded to overpower me and put a knife at my throat. I was five months pregnant and I remember vividly the flashing through my mind of a vision of myself lying dead on the floor and our baby dead. I remember almost fainting as he had his arm around my neck. I was out of breath. I also remember screaming "Don't hurt the baby. Don't hurt the baby." He got

---

Toni Napoli is a 45 year old Master's level therapist, currently working with women. She has resided all her life in the Northwest. She has been married for 21 years and has two children, ages 20 and 17.

© 1991 by The Haworth Press, Inc. All rights reserved.

me into the bedroom and committed sodomy and rape. He stole the $80.00 in cash I had in the house. At 11:30 a.m., he was gone, and so began the long, long road toward recovery. I looked outside the living room window with my bathrobe on and realized that the whole time this was happening, children were outside playing across the street on the elementary school playground. This really didn't happen; not during the middle of the day on a Monday, in my own home! It didn't really happen! I was in a daze. I was shaking, but I was able to call my father who worked nearby in the neighborhood. I also called my husband who worked further away. I quickly dressed before my father came. I have no idea why I did that, but I felt so dirty, so unclean. I had to cover up somehow. When my father came, we called the police, who promptly came to the scene. I remember vividly the policeman saying, "You mean this happened, and all those kids are across the street playing?" During the police interview, my mother arrived with an uncle. I remember she was extremely upset. After the police left, my husband, my mother, and I went to the medical clinic for an examination.

At the doctor's office, I was extremely worried, and kept asking about the baby. "Would the baby be okay?" "Would this trauma hurt the baby?" The doctors tried to reassure me that with all indications the baby should be all right.

The following months were quite traumatic. Knowing what I know now, we did all the classically wrong things after a trauma. We left our three bedroom home and moved in with my parents. A few months later, we lived with my grandmother, and a few months after that, we actually moved to a small town two hours away. It was quite a blow to my husband's ego that I would not even go back into the house with him in the evening; that I could not trust enough to have him by my side. I tried to make him understand, but I could not do it. In the following months, my husband, relatives, and friends stood by me and rallied around me. They also grew tired of me. I recall two months after the rape my parents wanted to go out for the day and I was petrified to stay alone. I literally had been babysat for two months. I remember so well the terror during the day. No more would the safety of daylight and the security of my own home ever feel the same. During those months, I did see a psychiatrist. He was a very nice, kind, good psychiatrist. He helped me work out immediate, awkward things, such as fear, and not wanting to have sex with my husband. He stated that this interracial rape may have been a racist act, that it is possible we were caught up in the civil unrest of the 1960s that was affecting Seattle and the rest of the country at that time. I never have considered myself a prejudiced person. It did not matter to me that the rapist was a Black man. It mattered to me that I would never feel safe again. Yet, it is true that in the subsequent years, Black men engendered more fear in me than White men, but *all* men were to be feared from that day on.

Our daughter was born in February of 1970. A happy, healthy baby girl. However, all my fears and anxieties were now projected onto her. Every move she would make, every time she would sneeze, I would jump. I was terrified something was going to happen to her. The veil of denial had been forever lifted, and I knew that bad things happen. I was hypervigilant. For if this bad thing happened, couldn't other bad things happen also?

However, we were getting into some semblance of normalcy with our baby daughter when one March evening the phone rang and it was the prosecuting attorney's office telling me that the court date had been set. Two months after my rape, the assailant had been apprehended for committing another rape. He had committed seven in all. I had experienced the painful experience at that time of picking him out in a line-up, and re-experienced the terror. Now it was time for the terror to surface again. Only this time, I had to experience the humiliation of being attacked by the defense attorney on the witness stand. He did not attack my sexual life, but he attacked my credibility in recognizing the assailant. By the time I left the witness stand, I was devastated. I ran into the hallway, where I was alone, and wept. My husband was in the courtroom listening to the testimony, and there was no one to comfort me after I was on the witness stand. The man who raped me was found guilty and was sent to prison for many counts of rape. That was a comfort to us that he was off the streets. But it was a small comfort, because I knew there were so many more assailants who would be attacking women.

It is hard to describe the years that followed. In June 1970, we moved to a small town on the coast of Washington. It was a drastic change. Now, I had left my total support system, all my family and friends, and had relocated to a small town that was hostile to new people. I knew absolutely no one. In addition to my raw terror at being home alone during the day, I had acute loneliness and difficulty adjusting to a new location. Somehow we survived that, and two years later had our son. My husband started up his first upholstery business. However, I was still very anxious about my children. My husband and I were fighting, and I was subject to temper tantrums and outbursts of rage. In 1974, we moved back to a suburb of Seattle where my husband started up his second business. Our lives took on a sort of normalcy. We still were prone to periodic and very emotional fights, but we were making a nice life for ourselves in suburban America. It seemed as though the rape was behind me. There were moments, especially when someone came to the door during the day, that I would panic. But aside from those times, I felt like I had put it behind me. That is, until January 1977, when I underwent another traumatic experience.

The telephone rang early on a Monday morning, and a man on the other end said he had our five year old son, and called him by name. It was quite odd, because I knew our son was sitting in the family room . . . at least I thought he was. Since our home was quite a long rambler, I ran all the way to the family room to find him sitting there. I got back on the phone, and the man on the line laughed at me. He said that I should be careful because he would get our son. Another trauma; another terror; another telephone call to my husband to come home at once; another phone call to the police. I even wondered at this time if it was the man who raped me, and if he was out of prison. Bizarre things were going through my mind. Who could it be? Who would know my son's name? Why would anyone do such a thing? We were under a siege of utter terror about our children. We did not get a babysitter or go out socially for months. We kept a close watch on them. We alerted our daughter's school and our son's preschool. We alerted all our friends and neighbors, while wondering if it was one of them. I was not sleeping, I was having severe infections. I was a wreck. About two weeks after this threatening phone call, it occurred to me that I was not just afraid of the phone call, although that was threatening enough, I was just as afraid that somebody was going to come to the door. I realized then that I was also experiencing leftover fear from the rape eight years prior. This was extremely overwhelming, confusing, and bewildering, because this could not be, it was eight years later . . . could it? I mentioned this experience to a friend and professional at our local Catholic church. She wisely directed me to Reverend Marie Fortune, a pioneer in her field. At that time, in 1977, Marie was founding the Center for Prevention of Sexual and Domestic Violence. She was housed in a small office in a church in Seattle. Her agenda was to work with sexual and domestic violence through the churches, to help the clergy help people. I saw Marie a few times and she was extremely helpful. She helped me understand the wrong that had been committed twice. She helped me address the fear. That summer of 1977 was one of the worst of my life. I was so needy, so desperate, and fighting with my husband all the time because he could not give me the comfort I needed. In the fall, we began marital counseling. The counselor wisely directed us to the local rape relief agency for specific trauma counseling, and we continued some marital counseling as well. From January to April, 1978, we went to weekly sessions at the rape relief agency. It was extremely helpful. I remember my husband and I looked at one another and said, "Where was this in 1969? My God we could have used it then!" Well, of course, it did not exist in 1969. It did not exist until 1975. The counselors at the rape relief agency had knowledge, sympathy, and helpful skills in working with the experience of the rape and the phone call. We were grateful to them and for their expertise.

At the same time that my husband and I were receiving help at the rape relief agency, I also enrolled in self-defense classes at the Feminist Karate Union. These classes were run by Py Bateman. She was a black-belt in karate, and formed the Feminist Karate Union to help women defend against rape. I took karate lessons for a whole year, and learned how to defend myself. The karate built my confidence. I had to find the violence in me to enable myself to strike back at an assailant. It was not just learning routines, blocks, and strikes, but it was also a process of looking deep within myself. When I graduated from the basic white-belt to the orange-belt, I discontinued the karate. It was not something I wanted to do forever, but it helped me gain a confidence that nothing else has done.

The Feminist Karate Union did a wonderful service for the City of Seattle. They taught self-defense to high schools, colleges, and women's groups all over the greater Seattle area.

To help others, and to continue my own recovery, I became a volunteer for King County Rape Relief in September 1978. Working for that agency as a volunteer was my first professional training, and it was a dramatic experience that would forever change my life. The training at King County Rape Relief was intensive. The group of volunteers met once a week for four hours a night for twelve weeks. We learned about rape trauma, the rescue triangle, and about counseling and operating the 24-hour crisis line. We learned about medical implications, and walking a victim through the medical system. We learned about the role of the police department, and how to walk a victim through a police interview. We learned about the prosecutor's office, and the prosecuting attorney. We learned about the judicial system, and the experience of court for the victim. We learned about family's and neighbors' reactions, and explored how to help them cope with the trauma and with the victim—knowing that the trauma happened to the whole family, not just the victim. At the end of the training, we were told by the agency that we were experts in sexual assault, that there was no one who knew more than we did. They were right. As a volunteer operating the 24-hour crisis line, I came into contact with many victims. They were all ages, sizes, and colors. Sometimes the victims were children and teenagers. After working the crisis line for a few months, the reality of women's lives became apparent to me. I learned that the assailants were not the only offenders, but also the police, the doctors, the judges, the attorneys, the newspapers, the next-door neighbors, the husbands, and the lovers. I saw how helping professionals would sometimes revictimize the victim. It happened more often than not. Classic remarks would be made: "Well, why were you out late at night?" or, "That is what happens when a teenager hitchhikes." If the victim happened to know her assailant, it was much worse for her. Then she was indeed under scrutiny from the police and the public. The professionals were much more understanding of "blitz rapes," which was the kind I experienced, than acquaintance rape. It was disillusioning for our group to realize how much education the professionals and the public needed about women being harassed and raped. Working for King County Rape Relief, I had experienced the bonding of women working in groups to help one another. I experienced the empathy that women have for one another, because we realize and experience the special pain and the special needs that other women have.

The experience at King County Rape Relief was also to have a profound effect on my personal life. When people are called into action and work for a cause, somehow that has to spill over into a learning experience for their personal lives. Indeed, this was the case for me in 1979. After nine months of working with King County Rape Relief my assertiveness, awareness, and consciousness definitely increased. I was finally able to face my husband's alcoholism. It had been suggested to me a few years previously, but I was in denial. Having faced my own rape trauma, having worked with other victims working through trauma, it was not possible to be in denial any longer about this trauma. I separated from my husband for the summer, saying I could not live with the drinking any longer. I sought help at Al-Anon. I realized that if the separation continued, I would have to support two children. I felt powerless and vulnerable, because I had been home taking care of the children for all those years. Yet, I was only a few credits away from my teaching degree, and was determined that I was going to be marketable and take care of myself and our children, so that I would never feel that powerless again. My husband and I did get back together, and he stopped drinking. I did go back to school, get my credentials, and began teaching. Understanding women's needs became a key concern in my life.

While teaching in a small Catholic elementary school, I met a priest who had rigid ideas about sexuality. He refused to let the teachers teach a sexual abuse curriculum to help the children. He was making inappropriate statements about the girls wearing short-shorts at soccer. He told the parents in a parents' club meeting that they should not allow their daughters to wear those shorts, that they would invite a rapist to attack them. He was openly stating the widely-held myth about sexual assault that blames the victim. I was horrified that this information would be coming from another helping professional, and even more horrified that it was coming from someone in the church. I was faced with the reality again that the assailants are not the sole offenders; they are also the priests, the people of the church. A direct confrontation with the priest did nothing but polarize us. Writing a letter to the archbishop even made more enemies. Now, what was I going to do about my faith, and what was I going to do about my job? Could I possibly continue working for this priest?

I decided that I would resign and study for a Master's Degree in counseling so that I could help women. It was not a coincidence that during the time I was teaching, my husband and I began therapy and realized that even though the alcohol was absent from our lives, emotional abuse was not. While I was teaching, I spent a couple of years attending a women's domestic abuse group. My husband spent the same amount of time in a men's anger management group. Through this excellent counseling, we were able to salvage our marriage and stop the abuse in our lives.

At the time I entered Seattle University to study for my Master's Degree, I had been through so much and learned so much that I had a ferocious desire to help women through therapy. Knowing that women are emotionally, verbally, physically, and sexually abused, I decided I would like to help, somehow, to stop abuse toward women in our society. While studying at Seattle University, I also worked for a cooperative mental health agency, where I received training in working with groups that were helping women. These groups included domestic and sexual abuse. I learned the theory of "learned helplessness" with women in abusive situations. I experienced the frustration of working with perfectly capable and able women who could take care of themselves in every way except that they would fall into "learned helplessness" with their husband. The reality was that women did not know there was any other choice. One of the priorities for the domestic abuse group was to show women there are choices other than being abused. While working with these groups, I learned about male dominance in abusive situations, and how in our society men are taught to express anger instead of allowing themselves to be vulnerable. I learned about co-dependency. Together, the women and I learned about the cycle of violence, and the continuum of violence. Women were amazed to discover that abuse can consist simply of critical remarks. It was helpful that I had experienced what the women in the group had experienced. I knew how they felt. I could empathize with the feeling of abandonment and the anxiety about separating from someone you love. I could identify with the fear of getting a job, and taking sole care of one's own children. As my own awareness expanded, my rage increased. Was there anywhere that a woman was safe? Was there anywhere in our society that a woman was respected?

Working with women who had survived child sexual abuse served to escalate my rage. In these groups, I heard the stories of how women were abused when they were tiny, little girls. I experienced women telling about blatant atrocities and horrible invasions of their bodies. Working with women sexually abused as children was a training ground that provided much information about women who suffer deep psychological problems stemming from their abuse. The term "borderline" often comes up in a mental health setting. How sad it was to realize that so many of these "borderline" women had been sexually abused when they were growing up. Doing these groups, I learned that the victim, as a child, develops defense mechanisms to survive. The defense mechanisms serve them when they are growing up, but hurt them as adults. In these groups, women broke through their denial and faced their incredible pain, their overwhelming anger. These women worked hard for recovery in the groups.

I was fortunate to have experienced working with domestic abuse groups and incest survivor's groups, and to have trained under Vicky Boyd, a pioneer in the field of domestic abuse. I trained, too, under Pat Nelson, who gently led me through working with sexual abuse groups.

However, all was not blissful doing women's therapy. In both agencies and private practice, many therapists disapproved of domestic and sexual abuse groups. Clinicians disagreed with the supportive kind of therapy and the empowering kind of therapy we advocated. It was then I learned that in mental health settings not everyone was going to agree with feminist therapy, or feminist ways of helping women.

Upon receiving my Master's Degree in 1988, I began working as a therapist in a Group Health Cooperative. My work has consisted of individual therapy, as well as women's issues support groups, women's domestic abuse groups, and groups for women who were sexually abused. My current caseload coincides with the national statistics: 40 percent of my clients are women who were sexually abused as children. Always, my goal is to help stop abuse of women and children, and to enhance the lives of women in the future.

It is not always an easy goal to try to make a better world for women. As a therapist, I run into roadblocks with my own colleagues in the mental health field, and I am sometimes astonished at the ignorance of otherwise sensitive, compassionate therapists. I run into obstacles when I am telling a client's story and a male therapist will say to me, "Do you believe that?" and I'll say, "Yes, I believe that this woman encountered all this horrendous sexual and physical abuse when she was growing up . . . of course, I believe it. Why shouldn't I believe it?" I find that some male therapists are uncomfortable with the information they receive from women and tend not to want to believe their stories.

What I learned in the mental health setting was not new. The assailants were also the mental health professionals. Some women have stories of further sexual abuse by their male therapists. I have learned that it is not easy being a feminist therapist. Nevertheless, I am determined to continue working with women.

Another area that I have chosen to work in is the Catholic church. I am currently the chairperson for the Women's Commission in the local Catholic Archdiocese. I mention this because it is another area where I am working with women, and it is another area that has been essential to my professional training. We are a group of women trying to make change in the Catholic church. We are a group of women listening to the voices of women in our diocese and advising the bishops accordingly. Often, it feels like we are symbolic more than productive; however, the symbolism is important. We believe in, and model, feminist process rather than male dominance. Through this group, I have learned the value of the feminist process, and the value of a consensual decision making model. I have taken my learnings from this group into my workplace and my personal life.

I have found that my feminist philosophy permeates my life. I feel power every time I am in a women's group and women are sharing their pain and telling their stories. This is what feminist therapy is—women sharing. Feminist therapy evolved because women needed to share their pain. It evolved because women's reality is different from men's reality. It evolved because women were being attacked, harassed, and abused. It is my hope that women in the 90s will have different stories than women in the 70s. I dedicate this manuscript to my daughter, who is now 20 years old, and who recently heard my story. I have high hopes for her and the women of the 90s.

On Remaining a Radical Lesbian Feminist While Training in Psychiatry

Laura L. Post

CHILDHOOD (1960-1978)

Born into a dysfunctional family dominated by strong individualistic women, I received many messages about gender inequity and the roles of women. My paternal grandmother, twice widowed, had supported herself selling lingerie. As a heavily made-up anorexic she presented the image, even into her 70s, of a successful business woman. Personally seductive, she spoke to men and giggled in their presence. Her gifts to my mother were flimsy items, lacier than my mother's tastes, yet a constant reminder that an athletic woman who wore pants and no makeup was "doomed" to motherhood or nursing/teaching/social work. My grandmother's material gifts to me — my choice at an elegant New York City toy store — underscored the economic triumphs earned by her wiles.

My maternal grandmother, by contrast, was a sturdy, short woman. Unlike my paternal grandmother, who could not cook (and mostly ate out), my mother's mother, also widowed, taught me the joys of eating healthily and well. Dismissed as "dumpy" by her rival grandmother, Nora was warm, physical, and loving. She had also graduated from Cornell University and pursued her PhD. Nora

---

Raised in New York City and educated in the Ivy League secondary school and university system, Laura L. Post has published in *Sinister Wisdom, Federation Proceedings, Hot Wire, Biochemistry and Cell Biology, Common Ground,* and *The Journal of Cell Biology*. She has two cats, Cleo and Raisin, and enjoys backcountry camping. She does writing, speaking, and workshops on women's culture, women's sexuality, women's health, and the roles of lesbian professionals.

© 1991 by The Haworth Press, Inc. All rights reserved.

still remains politically active, through the Grey Panthers, through her writing about ageism, through her mourning that, despite her aptitude and motivation, she had spent her life raising twins and not in a career as a lawyer, like her husband, brother, and son.

The only child of a career electrical engineer and another foiled woman lawyer, I saw a father whose work came first yet who expected dinner to be on the table whenever he came home. My mother remained powerless and frustrated in her attempts to feel respected. My father continually encouraged her to wear the nightgowns purchased for her by his mother, reinforcing the non-acceptance that my mother must have felt for not wearing makeup or frilly clothes.

Supported by my mother, I wore vests and sneakers to school. By dressing as I did, by being successfully athletic and "one of the boys," by being vocal about sexism through four years of mostly-male Ivy League New York City prep school, I was branded as a feminist long before I had seized the political import as my own. In excelling academically, I was treated as a genderless scholar or as a female to be flirted with, rarely with respect as a bright, sensitive woman.

COLLEGE (1978-1983)

Through high school and college, I found myself competing with males. Inundated with texts and prose written by men and teachers who were men, I felt the foreignness that Sonia Johnson has described "alien to me, hurts me, assaults me, offends me." Without women role models with whom I could easily identify, I found myself struggling for the first time with my beliefs in the utility and benevolence of higher education. I became more aware that the academic world in which I lived did not include many people of color, differently abled, or women in positions of herstorical or essential power. The prestige of the clubs was reserved only for men.

Moreover, there seemed to be a process in operation, not open to doubt or discussion, of how to best learn. Though my instincts were to group together and approach problem sets and reading assignments collectively, the reinforcement that I received was that singular superlatives were the goal, that collaboration placed my talents and contributions in question, that cooperation was akin to cheating. Taking in and regurgitating knowledge was the way. There was little processing of feelings. I desperately sought thoughtful, evolved people with whom to engage, and I experienced disappointment in the absence of the intellectual spirit I had hoped to find. I knew computer jocks, diligent, bland students who turned in "A" papers, and those whose avant-garde thinking occurred only late at night, over drinks, cigarettes, and coffee.

Though I had previously estimated my greatest talents to be in the creative arts, but believing that science offered the greatest challenge, and, therefore, reward, I found myself applying to medical school. A graduate school year abroad, with focus on French novels and theatre, had convinced me that professional life in literary academia would quickly erase the pleasures in reading and writing. Back in the United States, and working on my own project in a high-powered biochemistry laboratory, I discovered that competitiveness in scientific research had eviscerated my joy in theoretical thinking and discovery. Volunteering at an alternative community mental health center, I found that I liked and was good at telephone hotline counseling. I decided to become a psychiatrist.

My training as a hotline counselor focused on my own issues as well as on philosophical and practical topics. The training and supervisory processes were feminist in orientation: allowing each person respect and freedom to speak, acknowledging and affirming emotions, clarifying boundaries, taking responsibility for our own behavior. For the first time, the system of learning matched my concept and needs; as I grew, I assimilated facts and ideas that were bold, fascinating, and new to me.

Previously convinced that I was the equal of men and of women, I recognized, to my horror and shame, that, in the form of my "successes," I had blindly perpetuated the ongoing oppression of women by the patriarchy. My schooling, my relationships, my thinking had been based on values established by and for men. I felt sad and angry that powerful reinforcers by authority figures had prevented me from honestly, decently accomplishing my goals. I realized that my ideal (to be the best) had power dynamics built into it, and I began to reconstruct my life plan (to be as good as I could).

About the same time, I began hanging around women's bookstores, attending concerts and talks in the feminist cultural network, and talking about my feelings. I came out as a lesbian, affirmed and encouraged by my social group. I entered medical school in the summer of 1983, armed with a B.A. *magna cum laude* in Biology from Harvard University and a M.A. *magna cum laude* in French Literature from the Universite de Paris IV. I experienced regret at some of what I'd done to achieve those results. I harbored the firm intention of resisting and furiously educating about the sexism/homophobia/misogyny that I imagined I was to encounter in the midwestern, blue-collar city where I was heading.

MEDICAL SCHOOL (1983-1987)

During the first few months of medical school, I went to the heterosexual parties and felt alone, out of place. I began to question my lesbian identity in a way that I had not done while living in the rarified, supportive atmosphere in Boston. I heard of a gay man among the faculty and came out to him, seeking guidance about my career. He did not come out to me and, furthermore, warned me that being an openly lesbian psychiatrist was not only dangerous but narrow and suspect. I felt my hopes crumble.

It was difficult for me to divulge much of my personal life to peers in medical school. I secretly joined a task force of the national medical student organization, the American Medical Student Association (AMSA), called "Lesbian and Gay People in Medicine" (LGPIM). I missed my friends in Massachusetts.

At the regional October AMSA meeting that first fall, I attended the LGPIM task force, anxious at encountering someone I knew from medical school who would now reject me, fearful of meeting no one to whom I would be able to relate. I was surprised to see a woman I recognized from medical school, who came out at the meeting and came over to me afterwards. Though awkward to meet in such a convoluted way, she, as well as many of the people I met that day, became friends who eased my way through the rest of medical school.

Strengthened by the affirmation inherent in simply being with other lesbian and gay medical students, I felt encouraged to write reviews, in the medical school paper, of two workshops that I had attended. One, on Chinese Medicine, received little comment. The other, on taking a sensitive medical history, including nonjudgemental questions on sexual orientation and concerns, prompted my being grilled in the Dean's Office, unprovable academic discrimination against me, and my referral to a psychiatrist. [Seriously ill with mononucleosis during my first semester, I was not permitted, as were colleagues, to take fall makeups for the two classes that I failed. I was forced to remediate the two classes during the following summer, and a research grant that had been awarded to me for that summer was revoked.]

The psychiatrist, a psychoanalytically-trained heterosexual, white male, provided my first role model, albeit negative, of a therapist. During the course of our several months' work together, which I terminated abruptly after he made explicit his sexual attraction toward me, I learned that my academic "difficulties" would disappear if I would only agree to have included in my folder that my troubles were due to a problematic relationship with a man in Boston. I was, in fact, involved with a woman in Boston. Under duress, and with a great deal of hurtful self-denial, I did agree and succeeded academically through the remainder of medical school, graduating *cum laude*. I found out, subsequently, that similar sorts of discrimination had occurred with the lesbians in the two classes behind me.

Needless to say, my confrontation with the realities of the situation frightened me, and I withdrew from my attempts to be an out lesbian in the medical school context. For example, during my six-week clinical psychiatry rotation, I did not say anything when the topic of homosexuality-as-interrupted-development arose. I went on to win the prize as the outstanding medical student in psychiatry; I wonder if that prize would have still been awarded to me had my lesbianism been publicly known. Through my four years in medical school, despite thirty-six hour shifts and overnight call every third night, I attended every national and regional AMSA meeting and remained active in LGPIM.

Determined, still, to be an openly lesbian psychiatrist, I applied to postgraduate residency training programs in large cities only. Not wanting to enroll in a homophobic residency, I sent out openly lesbian applications. Some interviews were affirming to me personally, to my medical abilities, and to the unique talents and knowledge that I might bring to psychiatry because of my having worked through a large part of my identity. At other interviews, I was asked repeatedly whether I believed that my being a lesbian would interfere with my ability or inclination to treat "normal," "straight," "typical" patients. I was asked at most interviews what I thought had "made me a lesbian." Hopeful of an enlightened and appreciative environment for training, I selected a program in San Francisco.

During my final year in medical school, having been accepted to the residency of my choice, I became involved with the local women's newspaper collective. I began by interviewing a woman musician whose performances I had enjoyed and went on to produce a concert of her music. Working amidst this group was an experience that partially healed the wounds from my oppressive and abusive medical school experience and re-validated my own sense of intuition, the goodness of working with women, and that my emotional and other "non-rational" approaches were o.k., useful, and desirable.

For the first time since college, I felt solid as a lesbian, as a feminist, and as a woman, living in women's culture though working in a man's world and in a male-dominated profession. I believed that I would be able to function effectively as a lesbian psychiatrist.

PSYCHIATRY RESIDENCY (1987-PRESENT)

Hopeful and excited, I moved to San Francisco. I had made up my mind to learn what I wanted to know in an accepting, albeit mainstream, program. Though I professed the intention of being classically versed in traditional Freudian thinking, I hoped to be able and encouraged to integrate my firm feminist principles into psychiatric training. I envisioned applying collective processes, cooperation, and a non-hierarchical frame to my work with clients.

My first six months of the four-year residency training were spent in a psychiatric inpatient setting of a large general hospital. I had selected and been assigned to a ward which had an "AIDS Focus," including many gay/lesbian staff and patients with psychiatric presentations of HIV disease. In August, I went to the Michigan Womyn's Music Festival, an annual gathering of (predominantly lesbian) women in women-only space for days of music, cultural networking and political consciousness-raising. I had announced my vacation publicly at the ward meeting: the other lesbians on the team smiled knowingly, and the rest of the staff asked warm, curious questions. I felt welcome, accepted. It was a relief to be able to be myself at work, unadulterated, unedited, unapologetic.

I was permitted to run the team meetings non-hierarchically. This meant that I was not directive, that I expected each group member to participate without my reminder. I had explicitly stated my intended plan for the treatment meetings in advance and was met with support and delight by the female staff (nurses, social worker, occupational therapist), with reservation, concern, and doubt by the male staff (physicians). In fact, I was repeatedly taken aside and warned that disruption of the useful hierarchal meeting structure would eventually result in my failure. I thought that my system worked well, with time for our own feelings and process which were used not only as venting but as relevant clinical information about particular patients. And, to the credit of my (gay male) supervisor, though he found my method foreign and unacceptable, his final evaluation of me stated only that we had disagreed about leadership styles.

In my second year of residency, I worked in two other inpatient psychiatric settings that I found to be restrictive and emotionally dysfunctional. Looking back, I appreciate just how unaffirmed I felt there, in that the presentations I chose to give, in an attempt to be self-affirming, during those months, were on the topics of alcoholism in the lesbian community and alternative medicine (i.e., the use of herbs, acupuncture, crystals, and chakras which are all familiar to lesbians). As previously, I sought validation from personal endeavors: I began to write for a national lesbian magazine and went back to producing women's music and workshops.

I took four months off from work to solidify my own recovery from alcoholism. I experienced ignorance and rejection from many of my professional mentors and peers after I announced my leave of absence and intimated the reasons for it. By contrast, when conveying my temporary withdrawal from production and writing to the women's community, I experienced encouragement, understanding, and empathy. Though I had previously felt my lesbian feminist self integrated with my psychiatric work, I began to wonder at the increasing percentage of time I was spending in my nurturing, alternative culture. I began to see myself as a missionary from the healing lesbian world to the goal-directed and destructive mainstream world.

During my third year of residency, I was assigned one and sought out another lesbian psychotherapist to supervise some of my cases. Both women used self psychology in their practices and had studied it deeply. The attunement/interpretation mode of self psychology matched my own intuitive approach and was intellectually acceptable to me. It felt good to start my formal training as a psychiatrist in a comfortable environment. Yet, there were still, from other supervisors and advisors, queries about what I thought "caused homosexuality," comments about the "inappropriate informality" of my pressed corduroys, Birkenstocks, and brightly-colored turtlenecks, as well as assumptions about the sexual attitudes and behaviors of my gay and lesbian clients.

There were also difficulties in applying theory written from a male perspective, entrenched within a patriarchal medical psychiatric system, to my cases. Specifically, my appellation became a focus of debate. I, in feminist, non-hierarchal tradition, wanted to be called "Laura" by my patients. Despite many years of being addressed as "Dr. Post," even before I had graduated from medical school, I viewed that titular addressing of physicians as a superioritizing mechanism: few other professionals (and only those in male-dominated specialties) were called by their professional degrees, and the majority of other mental health workers (usually women) were called by their first names.

This was an old battle for me. As a medical student, I had found myself frequently allied with (mostly female) nurses in terms of treatment and managerial styles, at odds with the (mostly male) physicians who were my superiors, and, ostensibly, my teachers. As a resident, having heard the arguments in favor of my being called "Dr. Post" (that's the way it's done in medicine; it's not appropriate to be called "Laura"; the boundaries in psychotherapy need to be preserved by the professional distance), I elected to try it my way.

I kept the boundaries and provided a safe space through my attitudes of respect and empathy toward my patients. I made clear that those who wished to address me by my first name could do so and that those who were more comfortable with "Dr. Post" could use that. I have a few patients who call me nothing, several patients who call me "Dr. Post," and the majority of patients who call me "Laura." Perhaps I've spent more time in my sessions discussing the meanings of different appellations, but I feel proud that I have this aspect of non-hierarchy in my practice.

The question of self-disclosure, in San Francisco where the choice of a lesbian therapist is a viable and positive one, and where not infrequent encounters of lesbian/gay patients occur, has also pervaded. Repeatedly warned not to reveal anything factual or personal about myself, I was confronted by a lesbian patient who suspected that I might be a lesbian but who was seeking only an out lesbian therapist with the hope of working through some of her internalized homophobia. Referred to me specifically as a lesbian client, by a resident colleague who knew that I was a lesbian, I was at a loss as to what to do.

Though apparent to me that other issues were involved in this woman's treatment, I also felt that we had a significant therapeutic alliance and that allowing her to terminate with me and my training institute in search of an openly lesbian therapist in the community would not be the most helpful alternative. Aware that, should any difficulties arise from my decision to self-disclose, I would not be supported by my residency program, I did decide to come out to that patient. We spent several sessions looking at what this meant to her, and I think both of us felt relieved. The therapy has gone well, and we have run into each other at events (Gay Pride Day, women's music events) where, even had I not been willing to come out to her, she would have been confirmed in her sense that I was a lesbian anyway, just not the sort with whom she wanted to work.

Through my years of university, medical, and residency training I have had to deal with being both a visible (woman) and an invisible (lesbian) minority. At times, I have wanted to be more visible as a lesbian and have dressed and acted in ways commensurate with my intentions, often invoking distaste or wrath from unenlightened and unsympathetic authorities. Though such encounters might be labelled as acting out in traditional thinking, an alternative philosophy might just as easily recognize the self-expression of a sensitive, oppressed-minority person so crucial to self-esteem, identity, and solidarity. Through my own recovery, I had been exposed to modalities of treatment untaught by and antithetical to the traditional medical/psychiatric system. And, I have become aware that being a "good resident" (displaying unquestioning willingness to work over one hundred hours per week, to unthinkingly obey medical elders, to utilize emotionally distancing mechanisms as survival techniques) is destructive to the process of being a "healthy person" (being in touch with my feelings, speaking out in useful ways, questioning, thinking, working through).

I have repeatedly questioned my place in such a milieu and wondered if, had I chosen a non-medical counseling specialty, would I have found fault with that? regretted it? wished for the choice of prescribing medication? missed the ability to comprehend concomitant disease? I have tried to integrate my woman's perceptions, my lesbian culture, my feminist beliefs into a difficult and often oppressive establishment. I perform psychotherapy in a non-hierarchal setting. I struggle daily with an interpretative balance between seeing narcissistic injuries in and acknowledging inegalitarian reality for my patients. I speculate about "health" in some clients who mobilize affects and beliefs that I personally would label as sexist/abusive/offensive/unacceptable but in whom I'm told that this represents release and progress. I try to balance case presentations between more empathic and expressive narratives of life story and the more ritualized, intellectual recountings demanded by the traditional medical environment.

No longer willing to only bring the healing arts from my lesbian feminist culture into the mainstream of my psychotherapy, I am making different choices. As a lesbian in recovery, I see my pathway in channeling both psychiatric and self-help treatments more specifically to other women, to other lesbians, to my people. Having worked, as a physician and counselor, in lesbian/feminist settings, I know that, though this is a radical concept, medical care can be provided in a cooperative, non-hierarchal manner. I do not regret my medical knowledge; I would like, though, to never again use it to overpower, to control, to demean.

Mostly, I have realized that, in order to work effectively with others, I need to care for myself. I have learned, painfully, that the mainstream medical/psychiatric setting in which I find myself will not care for me, nurture me, really acknowledge or understand me. I still feel disappointment at those uninformed and complacent who comprise the mainstream medical setting. I feel more disappointed still at those gay and lesbian physicians, psychiatrists, psychotherapists I have encountered who do not experience their homosexuality as a different culture but only as a minimizable demographic. I feel disappointed at how few openly lesbian feminist role models I have had who demonstrated consistently radical thinking and affirming action. I feel disappointed that there is no cohesive cultural approach to psychological analysis and that many minority patients are subject to the confines of mainstream descriptions, diagnoses, interpretations. I feel most disappointed at myself for having been so long satisfied with meager and minimal efforts at toleration by my medical and psychiatric colleagues.

I dream of founding a center for substance abuse and other issues for lesbians, staffed by lesbians in recovery, in separatist space. I applaud the new research by Carol Gilligan suggesting that women perceive, think, and express differently than do men and have those patterns oppressed out of us, by men, during adolescence, simply because they are different, and, therefore, threatening. I delight in the discovery, by archaeologist Marija Gimbutas, of a peaceful, ecologically-minded, goddess-worshipping women's culture that flourished in 4500 B.C. I feel validated by recent surveys reporting that 81% of female medical students have experienced some significant form of sexual abuse and/or discrimination during medical school. I wonder how the medical world would be different had women, and not men, created it. I look forward to my time spent in women-only space, discussing these issues with other aware and concerned lesbians.

Yet, there is still knowledge that I want, experiences that I can only get in the mainstream because there is no lesbian feminist residency training. Despite attempts to evaluate each datum before storing it in my mind — is this patriarchal or is this universally true? — I am still being taught things vital to my accreditation which are dangerous to me and to the work that I want to do. I have some answers and many more questions. And, now, within a year of completing psychiatric education as a resident, I have reformulated my conflict: how can I continue to integrate what I have learned in my formal training into my lesbian feminist philosophy?

Feminism and Psychology: A Dangerous Liaison

Six Spoke Collective

INTRODUCTION

Feminism and psychology, we are discovering, do not easily go hand in hand. Having entered graduate school with different understandings of feminism, we each, in our own way, have been struggling to continue to evolve as feminists while we develop as psychologists. Our experience suggests that these two ways of seeing the world often conflict. To succeed in our graduate program, our feminist convictions frequently must be denied. This paper explores areas in which this has occurred, and presents one way we, as feminist psychology graduate students, have joined together to effect our graduate experience and reduce the tension between feminism and psychology.

THE CLASSROOM EXPERIENCE

In general, feminist concerns are treated as peripheral in all areas of our graduate training. For example, they are ignored or relegated to one or two lectures within any given course. Further, they are seen as outside the legitimate body of research on a given topic and, almost always, fail to be integrated fully into our professional training. Feminist concerns are dismissed as reflecting a limited perspective relevant only to women, while mainstream theories and

---

Members of the Six Spoke Collective (in alphabetical order) are: Janice Berman, Patricia Burgmeier, Jeanine Cogan, Lynn Parrish, Debra Srebnik, and Jacqueline Weinstock. The six authors are graduate students in the Department of Psychology, University of Vermont, John Dewey Hall, Burlington, VT 05405.

© 1991 by The Haworth Press, Inc. All rights reserved.

empirical work are viewed as relevant to all. This can be seen in the fact that the feminist perspective is always labeled as such when it is discussed. The mainstream perspective (i.e., the white-middle-class-heterosexual-male perspective) is never named; it is taken as the status quo. It becomes the yardstick against which all other perspectives are measured. When this yardstick is challenged in class by feminist graduate students, the challenge is often trivialized with comments such as, "Oh, there they go again." This serves to maintain the status quo by tuning out the content of the message and effectively silencing the dissent. The mainstream perspective is never silenced; no one says, "Oh, there *they* go again."

There are various ways in which faculty play a role in keeping feminism out of the classroom. Some professors discourage the exploration of work they are not familiar with, and feminist perspectives often fall into this category. Consequently, bringing feminism into the classroom becomes a constant struggle which diverts much personal energy. In some cases, the end result is that we as feminist students educate our peers and professors, but lose the opportunity to participate in dialogue and an equal exchange of ideas. This prevents us from building on what we already know.

Even when faculty are receptive to the introduction of feminist viewpoints in their classes, they do not necessarily support, initiate or facilitate the process. For example, if a student complains that only one perspective is heard, the onus often falls on that student to bring in other perspectives. The response usually takes the form of, "Find a couple of readings in your special interest area to share with the class." By responding this way, professors fail to take personal responsibility for integrating feminism into the classroom, and they keep it in the realm of a "special interest area."

The classroom experience with professors who consider themselves feminists is somewhat different, though they too have difficulty effectively integrating feminism and psychology within the classroom. While feminist issues are more apt to be addressed, they still tend to be relegated to one or two lectures rather than treated as a perspective that is always relevant. We get the sense that feminist professors, like feminist graduate students, are silenced by the negative labels attached to feminist perspectives. We imagine that they fear for their professional standing; we fear that this is what we have to look forward to in our own careers.

RESEARCH TOPICS

The same current that runs through our difficulties in the classroom is present in our struggle to address feminist research questions. While it is now acceptable to study women as a population, it is much less acceptable to pursue feminist research questions. Negative comments, lack of encouragement, and an absence of feedback have discouraged us from pursuing these questions. Often, faculty members try to enlist students to work with them on their own research projects. While some may not intentionally limit us to their research areas, the fact that they are not familiar with (or open to) new, unconventional, or unstudied topics leaves students little choice but to work on faculty's research interests. For example, if one of us was interested in studying feminist spirituality and its impact on social adjustment, we might be able to find faculty who were interested and willing to supervise us, but we would not be likely to find faculty with the expertise to facilitate our work. Because so often it is the feminist areas that faculty are unfamiliar with, this becomes a feminist issue.

Lack of immediate support is not the only barrier to pursuing feminist research questions. Selecting such topics has negative implications for our future as psychologists. Graduate students who explore feminist questions are immediately viewed as having very limited research interests. This is because feminism is still not recognized as a broad, overarching perspective that can be applied to all areas of study, but is rather taken to mean that we are interested in research areas traditionally associated with women. Due to this labeling process, we suspect we may not be considered for many types of research positions. The assumption is that we would either not be interested in a project that wasn't viewed as "feminist," or worse, that we would not be qualified for it because it was outside our area of expertise (i.e., women). Our focus on feminist issues leads many to conclude that we have selected our career paths in women's studies instead of in psychology. Women's studies, to them, is less valued than psychology; it is viewed as the "Home Ec" of the 90's.

This lesser value our colleagues place on "women's issues" and feminist research troubles us as we look to our futures in psychology. Feminist faculty members in our department are less respected than non-feminist faculty members. Further, the more a feminist faculty member makes feminism a part of her research and teaching, the less respect she is accorded. We imagine these attitudes will also limit us. If things continue as they are, our colleagues who now devalue our feminist perspectives will be in the positions to make the decisions that affect our careers. We envision them as members of the editorial boards of prestigious journals, grant funding agencies, and hiring committees at competitive universities.

RESEARCH METHODS

Research methods that often fit best with our feminist concerns are also devalued. Whether these methods are adapted versions of the experimental model or alternative methodologies, our goals are to be more respectful of participants, more interactive with participants, and less hierarchical. None of these things are easy to accomplish in our program.

The barriers to changing the experimental method are tremendous. Deviating from the traditional approach is both implicitly and explicitly discouraged. Rather than struggling to adapt the traditional method, some feminists choose qualitative methodologies. While we recognize that any method can be used for feminist (or non-feminist) purposes, qualitative methods more easily allow us to respect participants' perspectives and thus may be more consistent with feminist philosophies. Unfortunately faculty tend to be unfamiliar with qualitative methodologies. Consequently, support for this work is often lacking. In addition, qualitative research is less valued than quantitative research. In sum, unless we use strictly traditional methods, we face the limits of our professors' experiences, journal preferences for quantitative procedures, and funding criteria.

CLINICAL TRAINING

Feminist perspectives are not well integrated into our clinical training. We now have one course on Feminist Therapy; however, most of the focus of our training is on traditional therapeutic techniques. While there is much room for feminist analysis within these frameworks, this does not usually occur. The societal context of oppression is rarely discussed in clinical supervision, nor is it introduced as part of therapy. As examples, while multiple role stress, sexual harassment, and assertiveness are all potentially fruitful areas to explore in the context of therapy with women, such areas often remain unexplored. The focus is on the individual; consequently, the societal context which has contributed to, and often largely caused, the "disorder" is ignored. In general, clinical training focuses on examining and changing the individual while feminism focuses on societal transformation.

Even when our supervisors allow for (or we ourselves introduce) feminist issues as part of therapy, rarely is the feminist perspective used to truly guide interventions. For example, during one intervention with women who had body image disturbances, it was acceptable in initial sessions for a feminist perspective to be examined. However, after these introductory sessions, the "real" intervention focused on challenging these beliefs, with no further recognition of the societal context of oppression. In essence, the women's experiences of oppression were denied.

In addition to the lack of feminist content in our clinical training, there is also a lack of feminist process. It is rare that any changes in the structure of therapy training occur as the result of feminist critiques. For example, in the supervision process, we have questioned the hierarchical nature of most therapies, where the client is seen as someone with few resources who needs to be "fixed" by the expert therapist. We have also questioned the emphasis on pathology, the need for diagnosis, and the reliance on a medical model of mental illness where the problem is perceived as "in" the individual. These questions are not often heard, and even when they are they still do not change the way we are expected to do therapy. We still must operate within the structural constraints of our clinical placements and supervision.

While the structural constraints make it difficult to integrate feminism into our clinical training, we also experience barriers at a more personal level. To develop an identity as feminist therapists, we need to have an understanding of ourselves as therapists and of the process of therapy. Developing this identity is not an explicit part of our program. Although it provides students the freedom to tap into many different resources, paradigms, and training settings, we lack support in our search for an identity as clinical psychologists. Without a vision of therapy that promotes healthy change and an image of how it may be accomplished, we are not in a position to integrate feminism into the traditional therapies we are exposed to.

MENTORS

Given this difficult environment, the need for mentors is acute. We need people who can support our efforts to integrate feminism into our professional and personal lives. In other words, what we need is both academic and personal. We need to be able to compare our struggles with the struggles our mentors have gone through in incorporating feminism into their lives and careers. We recognize that compromises are necessary to survive as feminists. What we want is to be able to discuss these compromises and to understand the contexts in which they were made. With this more personal understanding of our mentors we would be able to incorporate their experiences into our thinking.

Closely related to this need to know our mentors is our need for our mentors to know us. Unless they know our priorities, goals, and the areas where we are or are not willing to compromise, it is not comfortable sharing our struggles and concerns. Only in the context of a mutual relationship will their advice be based on our priorities and goals. For example, a mentor might advise us against doing too much feminist research in graduate school. This might be wise advice in general since we've seen that doing such research decreases our status as researchers. However, the advice might not be relevant if research is the one area in which we are not willing to compromise.

Unfortunately, the model for mentorship just described does not exist and would be difficult to implement in our graduate program. As it is usually women who are the advisors of feminist students, it is also a model that is likely to put extra demands on women faculty. We realize, too, that conversations about choices and compromises are problematic, especially when mentor and student opt for different choices. Still, we think such a mentor-student relationship is invaluable to the process of maintaining our feminism as we enter into our chosen profession. We also see this model as fitting well with feminist ideologies.

CONCLUSION: THE ROLE OF SUPPORT GROUPS

As illustrated in this paper, integrating psychology and feminism in our graduate training remains a great challenge. Individually, we have experienced sadness, frustration, hopelessness, and anger. We have been misunderstood, misinterpreted, silenced, and ignored. Several of us have seriously entertained the notion of dropping out of our program because of the profound isolation we have experienced. One thing that has sustained us, however, is coming together in mutual support in the form of a women's issues group. Through this group, we've begun to meet the challenges we face. Our group has served as a forum to share our struggles as feminists. It gives us the opportunity to validate each other's experiences, to explore frustrations, and to develop productive and feminist ways to function within a constraining institution. By listening to each other's stories, we are reminded that the problems we encounter often stem from the larger system rather than from the individual. Together we still experience sadness, frustration, hopelessness, and anger, but we are able to explore these feelings, and to act from them.

While our group has been a positive experience, creating and maintaining it has been a struggle. Initially we focused mainly on maintaining cohesion at the exclusion of a more thorough analysis of our different assumptions about feminism and psychology. We came together wanting a safe place to be feminists because we had no other place to experience that safety. The process of writing this paper has helped us to talk about this need, to address our fears about disagreements, and to begin to explore our differences. We have learned much, and are now able to work together to support each other within the group and to move outside the group to positively effect our graduate experience. While we still experience sadness, frustration, and especially anger, we are no longer, at least for the time we come together in the late afternoons, misunderstood, misinterpreted, silenced, or ignored. Undeniably, we are not alone.

Graduate Training and Feminism: Maintaining an Identity

Melissa J. Perry

I can clearly remember the period of my development when I thought that the term "feminist" was a bad word. If someone mentioned feminism, my mind would automatically fill with classic stereotypes of bra-burning women who hated men. Declaring myself a feminist among my group of peers would have been akin to declaring myself a terrorist. But that was when I was an adolescent, still in high school, and experiencing a world that did not extend further than the physical boundaries of my working class rural community.

As uneasy as it makes me feel to admit it, college was responsible for changing my understanding of what it meant to be a feminist. Admitting this is uncomfortable for two reasons. The first is my disbelief in the notion that formal education makes one a better person. My versatile circle of friends and family, many of whom may be considered "uneducated" by college standards, is too intelligent and creative for me to believe that they should have gone to college. The second reason I feel so uneasy about this statement is because the relationship between feminism and formal education is too complex to be interpreted lightly. In fact, whereas the college experience was responsible for cultivating my feminist insight, the graduate experience is actually working to stifle that very same consciousness. In the next few pages I hope to untangle some of the intricacies of the relationships between graduate training, becoming

---

Melissa J. Perry received her BA in Psychology from the University of Vermont in 1988 and her Master of Health Science (MHS) from The Johns Hopkins School of Hygiene and Public Health in 1989. She is currently in her second year of doctoral research in the area of adolescent AIDS prevention.

a mental health professional, and maintaining a feminist identity. I will attempt to do this by following the course of my feminist development through three distinct phases, each of which has been directly influenced by different levels of academic education.

BEFORE FEMINISM

The period before feminism was during my adolescence, when the idea of feminism was completely frightening. It was frightening because in my community women were automatically considered inferior. Having a career or pursuing higher education was not desirable. My family and all of my friends' families were working class and working class to us meant that in the case of two-parent families, men were the bread winners and women were the mothers. Sometimes women worked, usually in factories, but only in order to subsidize the family income, the women never earned more than men. In the case of single-parent families like mine, women had to work but they still never earned more than their male co-workers. After all, we thought, men held the power and women were responsible for maternal and domestic support. Men always had the ultimate rule.

These traditional patterns often resulted in serious social consequences. Teen pregnancy was rampant among my female peers. I remember being present for the delivery of my best friend's child. She was 16 and it was too scary for either one of us to comprehend. Domestic violence was a big problem too, usually directly fueled by alcohol abuse. It seemed that women were "accidentally" hurting themselves a lot in my town. But the truth was, they never left. In retrospect I realize that few of those women ever knew where to go or what to do.

At the time, I observed my environment and learned important lessons about what it meant to be female. The first rule was that women existed in order to be attractive for men. Attractive meant not only physically (although that was very important) but also sexually and emotionally. To be attractive for men emotionally meant to be weak, acquiescent, accommodating, and naive. The second rule was to never feel too good about oneself. Now this rule was not intended to be followed only by females—men tended to have low self-images too—but we women always knew how important it was to be self-deprecating. We silently understood that we were somehow supposed to preserve any bit of self-esteem that our men might have and we did this by subordinating ourselves.

I realize now that the negative self-concept that most of the members of my community had was imbedded in our social class identity. We knew we weren't really cutting it when it came to comparing ourselves to the images of the American Dream. Our families were barely making a living, let alone achieving material success. Basic needs like paying rent and buying food were more important than worrying about self-enhancement. And when one is confined to dealing with issues of survival, higher-order thinking usually becomes clouded.

Although I internalized many of these cultural standards, I realized early on that I had some sort of desire to be different. I remember feeling the strong need for attention from males but I wasn't very good at playing the meek and innocent role. So I started to engage in "masculine" behaviors in order to make powerful statements. Drinking and fighting were my two favorites because they always won a lot of attention. I built a reputation for myself as a tough party-goer who wasn't afraid of anyone. This image made me popular with the boys because I acted like "one of the gang" and I realize now how it served a dual purpose: I was popular with the boys but I didn't have to compromise myself by acting out the stereotypic female role. Although I don't remember consciously thinking that I was rebelling against sex role inequities, it makes a lot of sense to me now. I never questioned the imposed inferiority of women; I just wanted to somehow be different.

Ironically, I always succeeded in school; achieving good grades was one of the most important goals in my life. I suppose I personally valued being smart but I knew it wasn't an attribute that made one popular among male peers. So I played out this double identity of honor student and party girl throughout high school until I was accepted to the state university. The transition into college, however, meant leaving a lot of my aggressive behaviors back home, along with my male party buddies. Having left these impediments behind, entering a new and very different environment, I was then free enough to discover my feminist consciousness.

THE DISCOVERY

Feminism was not the very first thing I discovered when I entered college, however. I learned other important lessons first, such as what it meant to come from a "nontraditional" background. I all too quickly interpreted nontraditional as being synonymous with working class and I discovered that few of my classmates could actually relate to the working class. That really didn't bother me as much as did realizing how important money actually was to most of my college peers. Many of the students I knew had come to college in order to obtain high paying jobs when they graduated. Most were very career-oriented. Moreover, the huge discrepancy between in-state and out-of-state tuition was my first clue about how much money these students' parents had.

I mention money because of its direct relationship to the predominant female "co-ed" identity I first learned about in the dorms. Unlike my high school experience, this was the environment in which material standards and femininity were tightly meshed. Here, I learned that to be female meant to be beautiful and being beautiful meant having nice things. Clothes were incredibly important as were jewelry, make-up, and hairstyle. Of paramount importance though was the size of one's body. Any slight trace of fat was revolting: a sign of ugliness and/or weakness. Whereas teen pregnancy was rampant back home, eating disorders were rampant in the dorms. The women were continuously dieting, always struggling to maintain control over food intake, calculating and recalculating calories. For the first time I learned to hate my body, my face, my hair and especially my cheap old clothes.

Given these experiences, I think I was truly ready for some kind of liberating discovery and that discovery came in the form of an undergraduate course entitled "The Psychology of Women." I entered the course still thinking that feminism was a bad word but I was excited about the psychology aspect since that was my major. Besides, I thought, the course could be used to fulfill an academic requirement. During the first day of class the professor asked us to write down what we hoped to get out of the course and how we felt about the status of women. I wrote that I thought there was no problem with the status of women. Each of us put our thoughts into an envelope and sealed it, only to be opened again on the last day of class.

Little did I know that this course would actually change my life both personally and professionally. Through course readings, journaling, and class discussions, I began to discover the feminist consciousness I had always unknowingly had. We began with simple topics like the use of language and the socialization of gender identities. Although I had known that females were treated differently and generally considered inferior to men, I realized for the first time that I didn't know *why* this was true. Then we discussed heavier issues like sex-role stereotyping and psychopathology in women. It was then that I realized the damaging effects that subordination was having on us.

I began to piece together my experiences at home and at college. I thought about the battered women in my town and the bulimic women in my dorm. I thought about how much I used to strive for male attention and how the beauty ideal I had recently internalized had destroyed any self-esteem I may have had beforehand. Then I made what was perhaps the most important discovery of all: It didn't have to be this way and I could do something about it.

I realized that I could do something about it by liking myself; liking my face, my hair, *and* my body. I could start enjoying being around other women as friends rather than as adversaries. I could stop stifling the empathic and nurturing side of my identity that I had buried so deeply as an adolescent. Most important, I realized I could do something about female oppression by educating myself, living daily life in a nonsexist way, and working to raise the awareness of others.

The Psychology of Women class' effect on me parallels in a way how a feminist therapist might affect a client. I identified areas of my own psychology which I felt were unhealthy (most of them related to insecurity and self-hatred), and I sought ways to alter these feelings through cultivating my feminist consciousness. It soon became clear that most of the other women I knew also felt they were inferior, incompetent and most often dependent. It was almost as if feeling insecure was a prerequisite for being female. Feminism helped me to stop hating myself and to start challenging the forces which had perpetually taught me and numerous other women the importance of passivity.

I was careful not to dive in too quickly or to become too radical because I feared not being taken seriously. I never started hating men directly; I just hated the privileges to which they were so automatically entitled. I believed that change had to occur for both sexes. I didn't blame women for being unaware nor did I blame men for being ignorant. I was hopeful, however, that change could and would occur. It just meant working together. In retrospect, I think I was being overly optimistic.

Since psychology was my major, I felt that it would be an ideal area through which I could achieve change as a professional. The psychology department had an exceptional feminist perspective and male professors rarely used sexist pronouns while speaking. Although the male tenured professors outnumbered the females, that pattern was slowly changing. Other psychology courses such as abnormal and developmental psychology included subsections on sexism and sex-roles. My Psychology of Women professor was conducting exciting research focusing on women and I was able to work as a research assistant for her. This experience influenced me to consider graduate training because I was realizing how important feminists could be for the future of research in psychology. Confining women to such subheadings as "women's issues" was too minimizing. A nonsexist or, even better, feminist orientation was what psychology needed. And I was ready to embrace that professional perspective.

THE STRUGGLE

The transition to graduate school involved learning more important lessons but the discoveries I have made here have been far less positive. In fact, somehow I have found myself in an environment that is quite opposite from the empowering experience I had in college. Initially I thought I had chosen the wrong place to pursue a career in research psychology, however I have come to understand it on a much deeper level. Namely, integrating feminism and professionalism involves serious struggle.

My graduate institution is oriented predominately toward research; both faculty and students maintain a work pace much like that of a treadmill. Actually, it seems to me that the name of the game here is keeping up, staying productive, and *always* working toward publication. In fact, publishing is what it's all about; not teaching, not mentoring, and definitely not solving social problems.

It is easy to equate the pace here with that of a corporation that values competitiveness, lack of emotionality, and hunger for success, even at the expense of others. It seems obvious to me how all these traits are more often valued by men than by women. I believe that this type of personality is often contrary to how women want to treat others or how they want to be treated. Yet, once again we are faced with the dilemma of either adopting traditionally "masculine" values or "choosing" failure. Most of my women professors and fellow graduate students are trying their hardest not to fail.

I believe these are the reasons why so few of my colleagues have a feminist awareness. It is easier to be asexual in an environment controlled by men than it is to identify oneself as a woman. I think too many women here have already learned this the hard way, as I am learning it now. We don't actively discuss instances of sexism because too much would be at stake to make such announcements public. Similarly, we don't challenge male professors to think or teach in nonsexist ways because they become too easily angered. After all, they would think, what does sexism have to do with my career anyway?

Now I don't mean to portray my graduate experience as being filled with instances of misogyny and direct oppression. It's not like that at all. Rather, issues relating directly to women, sex-roles, sexism, or feminism are just simply ignored. We all prefer to operate under an imaginary, asexual cloud which is usually guaranteed not to interfere with our productivity. By maintaining this pretense, we don't have to deal with uncomfortable issues like why there are only male professors in the department, or why our research findings often show significant gender differences for rates of psychopathology, alcohol and drug abuse, or why women are not being more heavily targeted for AIDS preventive interventions.

I initially wanted to blame all of my women professors and contemporaries for tolerating this kind of environment. I was angry at them for not being more active or vocal. But I realize now that that was a naive perspective to take. If anything I think I need to blame the "old boy network" for perpetuating this silence. Yet, most of all, I think I need to maintain some semblance of optimism. Although that elevated sense of self-esteem I achieved at college has weakened since I entered graduate school, I have definitely not abandoned my belief in women nor my belief in the possibility of change. I remember telling one of my friends in college about the all-male departmental faculty I would be facing at graduate school. She responded enthusiastically with "Well that's why you have to go there and straighten things out!" How I long for that kind of support now.

Nevertheless, I continue to live my daily life with a feminist perspective and I constantly watch out for instances in which I can tactfully provide feminist insight to both fellow graduate students and even sometimes professors. One conflict I have yet to resolve however is whether I will be able to face life as a professional if I am continually expected to stifle my feminist activism. I hope it is not a false belief that I only have to compromise myself now and play the game because of my impotent position as a graduate student. Once I enter the professional world it is my deepest hope that I will attain a position in which I can influence the feminist consciousness of others. And it is that hope which keeps me going.